ELECTROENCEPHALOGRAPHICS:
A NOVEL MODALITY
FOR GRAPHICS RESEARCH

Von der Carl-Friedrich-Gauß-Fakultät

der Technischen Universität Carolo-Wilhelmina zu Braunschweig

zur Erlangung des Grades eines

Doktoringenieurs (Dr.-Ing.)

genehmigte Dissertation

von

Maryam Mustafa

geboren am 20. Feb. 1982

in Pakistan

Eingereicht am:	05. Juni 2015
Disputation am:	13. Juli 2015
1. Referent:	Prof. Dr.-Ing. Marcus Magnor
2. Referent:	Prof. Dr. Douglas Cunningham

(2015)

Maryam Mustafa:

Electroencephalographics: A novel modality for graphics research

© 2015 Maryam Mustafa

Satz und Umschlag: Maryam Mustafa

Illustrationen: Maryam Mustafa

Herstellung und Verlag: BoD – Books on Demand, Norderstedt

ISBN 978-3-7386-4023-6

Bibliografische Information der Deutschen Nationalbibliothek:

Die Deutsche Nationalbibliothek verzeichnet diese Publikation in der Deutschen

Nationalbibliografie; detaillierte bibliografische Daten sind im Internet über

http://dnb.dnb.de abrufbar.

Contributions of the Author

Clarification of my individual contributions to the publications that describe parts of my thesis; The papers are ordered according to the structure of this thesis.

1. Maryam Mustafa, Lea Lindemann, Marcus Magnor. **EEG analysis of implicit human visual perception**. In Proceedings of the SIGCHI Conference on Human Factors in Computing Systems, pages 513-516, 2012

   I developed the ideas and experimentation implemented in this paper. L. Lindemann and I discussed ideas for artifact selection, data analysis and experimental setup. The paper was written and presented by me. M. Magnor guided the project with many suggestions and gave advice concerning ideas and content of the paper. The contributions of this paper are part of Chapter 3.

2. Maryam Mustafa, Stefan Guthe, Marcus Magnor. **Single-trial EEG classification of artifacts in videos**. ACM Transactions on Applied Perception (TAP), 9(3):12, 2012.

   This paper was selected as one of the best 3 papers of the ACM Symposium on Applied Perception (SAP 2012) conference and therefore was accepted by and published in the TAP journal. It was presented at SAP 2012. The ideas presented in this paper are part of Chapter 4 and all experimental work, data analysis and paper writing was done by me. S. Guthe was responsible for the wavelet based classification.

3. Maryam Mustafa, Marcus Magnor. **ElectroEncephaloGraphics: Making Waves in Computer Graphics Research**. Computer Graphics and Applications, IEEE , 34(6):46 - 56, 2014.

This paper was selected for a special issue of the Computer Graphics and Applications Journal on The Next Big Thing. I was responsible for the ideas, conducting the experimental work, data analysis, creating the neuro-feedback loop and writing the paper. Contributions from this work are presented in Chapter 5. Parts of this work are based on earlier work (Chapter 4) with S. Guthe who supported me with advice and suggestions for the implementation and evaluation of the algorithms. He was also responsible for the wavelet based classification. M. Magnor oversaw the project.

Summary

Neuroimaging and brain mapping techniques can provide meaningful insights and guidance for graphics related problems. This is particularly true given that most of the output from graphics algorithms and applications is for human consumption.

In this thesis I present the application of ElectroEncephaloGraphy (EEG) as a novel modality for investigating perceptual graphics problems. Until recently, EEG has predominantly been used for clinical diagnosis, in psychology, and by the brain-computer interface (BCI) community. Here, I extend its scope to assist in understanding the perception of visual output from graphics applications and to create new methods based on direct neural feedback. My work uses EEG data to determine the perceptual quality of videos and images which is of paramount importance for most graphics algorithms. This is especially important given the gap between perceived quality of an image and physical accuracy.

This thesis begins by introducing the fundamentals of EEG measurements and its neurophysiological basis. Following this introduction, I present a novel method for determining perceived image and video quality from a single trial of EEG data in response to typical rendering artifacts. I also explore the use of EEG for direct neural feedback and present a neural-feedback loop for the optimization of rendering parameters for images and videos. I conclude with an outlook on what the future of EEG in graphics may hold.

Zusammenfassung

In dieser Arbeit präsentiere ich die Anwendung von Elektroenzephalografie (EEG) als eine neuartige Modalität zur Untersuchung von Wahrnehmungsfragen in der Computergraphik. Bisher wurde EEG vorwiegend für die klinische Diagnostik, in der Psychologie und in der BCI-Community verwendet. Ich erweitere den bisherigen Anwendungsbereich um die Untersuchung von perzeptueller Qualität bildgebender Verfahren auf Basis von neuronalem Feedback.

Da die Ergebnisse der meisten graphischen bildgebenden Verfahren für die Betrachtung durch Menschen bestimmt sind, ist bei der Bildsynthese neben der physikalischen Genauigkeit ebenso die durch den Betrachter tatsächlich wahrgenommene Qualität von großer Bedeutung. Um die tatsächliche wahrgenommene Qualität von Videos und Bildern zu ermitteln, setze ich in meiner Arbeit mit EEG gemessene Daten ein.

Diese Arbeit beginnt mit einer Einführung der Grundlagen der EEG-Messungen und ihrer neurophysiologischen Basis. Nach dieser Einführung stelle ich eine neue Methode zur Bestimmung wahrgenommener Bild- und Videoqualität vor. In diese Methode ermittle ich ein Maß für die wahrgenommene Bildqualität, in dem die EEG-Daten von Probanden als Reaktion auf typische Rendering-Artefakte aufgezeichnet werden. Weiterhin erforsche ich die Nutzung des EEG für direktes neuronales Feedback und präsentiere eine Neuronale-Feedback Schleife zur Optimierung von Rendering-Parametern für Bilder und Videos. Ich schließe diese Arbeit mit einem Ausblick auf die zukünftigen Möglichkeiten, die das EEG der Computergraphik bereitstellen könnte.

To Halah,

my parents and in memory of Haroon

Acknowledgments

While the contribution of this dissertation is my own, I wouldn't have been able to finish it without the support of many.

I would like to express my sincere thanks to my advisor, Marcus Magnor for his constant support, ideas and all the valuable and constructive comments during each step of this work. Without his guidance, understanding, feedback and often times compassion this work would truly not have been possible. Thank you Marcus.

I would also like to thank Douglas Cunningham for always making the time for discussions about my work and for being the voice in my head cautioning me and expecting a stricter standard of scientific research. For that I am a better researcher and truly grateful.

Stefan Guthe also deserves my gratitude not only for his help in my work but for being the sounding board for my ideas and for always having a solution to my mathematics related problems.

I would like to express my very great appreciation to present and former colleagues of the Computer Graphics Lab at TU Braunschweig for creating a wonderful work environment. In particular, I would like to thank Martin Eisemann, Felix Klose and Kai Ruhl for the 'interesting' discussions in the kitchen and the endless hours of entertainment. Thanks Anja Franzmeier for supporting me not only in the administrative work but making me feel welcomed in this department and country. Thank you Carsten for maintaining all computers and solving many technical problems.

Further thanks goes also to my student assistant Julia Duczmal for her endless patience in the midst of all the EEG experiments.

Given that there exists a world beyond doctoral research work, I would like to thank my adopted family, the Prekazi's and Tahera, for being there through the good and the bad and for making me feel less alone. Thank you Ariana for being friend, sister, baby-sitter, aunt, therapist and so much more.

Many other friends have also provided support through the years. I can't name all of them individually, but I appreciate every single one of them. In particular, I'm grateful to Asli, Ghadah and Jeanne for providing me with a certain sense of normalcy and sanity in the last months of this work.

Finally, I would like to thank my family for the support they provided me through my life. Particularly, my parents who have been a constant support in everything I have achieved. I would especially like to thank Fatima for dropping everything to always be there so I could do my work. Thank you.

A very special thanks goes to Halah for being my partner in the many ups and downs of this journey. Only she can truly comprehend the toll of this journey and only she can truly appreciate its culmination in this work.

Contents

1. Introduction

"All our knowledge has its origins in our perceptions."

— Leonardo da Vinci

The ultimate purpose of computer graphics is to produce images and videos for human observers. Thus the success of any graphics application depends on how well it conveys relevant information to a human viewer. However, the inherent complexity of the physical world and limitations of computing hardware make it an impossible task to replicate the view of the real world. In fact, over 150 years of research on perception shows that no organism has a perceptual system that tries to create an exact representation of the real world. All perceptual systems, including the human perception system, make many assumptions in order to make sense of the real world. This can often lead to a gap between how we perceive the world and how it really is. Take for example the Café Wall illusion (Fig.1.1) where our perceptual system convinces us that the walls are not parallel when in fact they are. Given the vastly complex task of creating physically accurate imagery the best that graphics algorithms can aim for is to create perceptually accurate images. To achieve this goal it is essential to understand and analyse how the Human Visual System (HVS)

Figure 1.1.: The Café Wall illusion first discovered by Gregory and Heard
deceives the human perceptual system that the lines are not parallel [GH79].

perceives the world around it. This understanding will allow computer graphics
practitioners to take advantage of the flexibility and robustness associated with
human perception to decrease the gap between hardware performance and
desired performance. In rendering, for example, resources can be allocated to
areas of a scene that matter most to human observers, saving computation time.
Similarly, visualization techniques have benefited from perceptual measures
such as processing speed, which determines how quickly humans perceptually
process features such as colour and texture. The integration of methods and
techniques from perception research into graphics is particularly important
if the goal is to create realistic imagery for movies, games, and immersive
environments.

The study of perception is, however, a complicated task. The main difficulty
is that it can not be directly measured or observed. Given this, the only way to
study human visual perception is through indirect measures. Any perceptual

process does, to a certain extent, influence human behaviour and it is through the study of this behaviour (covert or overt) that we can create models of perceptual systems.

One of the main methodologies used by perception researchers to study and understand hidden perceptual processes are psychophysical experiments [MBB12]. Psychophysics is the empirical study of the relationship between physical stimulus and the resulting perceptual or sensory responses [Ges13]. It was first introduced in Fechner's Elements of Psychophysics which presents methods and theories for studying sensation [Fec48]. Psychophysical experiments are conducted in a highly controlled environment with an absolute control over as many factors as possible. Because of the desire for absolute control over the experiment, most psychophysical experiments use simple abstract stimuli. This makes it difficult to not only conduct these experiments but also to model the results.

Another technique typically used for perceptual research is the eye-tracker. Researchers have employed eye-trackers to investigate what kind of visual information people focus on while viewing images, videos, or visualizations. This can provide valuable information on which parts of the stimulus are important and on the order in which an image is scanned. These tools have become part of mainstream graphics research and have provided unique insights.

Brain imaging techniques are another class of measurement methodologies used for studying perception. Neuroimaging technologies allow researchers to visualize the processing of information in the brain directly. There are a number of safe imaging techniques in use throughout the world for research and medical purposes. Functional magnetic resonance (fMRI) works by detecting the changes in blood oxygenation that occur in response to neural activity. Technological advances in the acquisition of fMRI data and its processing have made it possible to analyse neural activity as quickly as the images are acquired allowing this data to be fed back to the subjects. It is then possible for subjects to voluntarily learn to modulate their own brain activity using real-time fMRI data (rtfMRI) [BHVH12]. Other signal acquisition techniques include magnetoencephalography (MEG) where brain activity is mapped by recording magnetic fields produced by electrical currents occurring naturally in the brain using very sensitive magnetometers. However, one of the most popular brain mapping techniques is Electroencephalography (EEG) which measures the electrical activity of large numbers of neurons close to the brain surface. EEG has been particularly important for sleep research and for detecting abnormalities in brain waves [RK87, FKH67, GAL90]. EEG has been used extensively in clinical psychiatry, brain-computer interface (BCI) research and perception due to its high temporal resolution, inexpensiveness and ease of use compared to the other imaging techniques.

Although psychophysical experiments and eye-trackers have been used extensively in graphics research, neuro-imaging methods have not yet been explored within a graphics context. Most neuro-imaging techniques have been used predominantly for medical diagnostic purposes, in perceptual psychology, and by the brain–computer interface (BCI) community to assist or augment human cognition and movement. Much of this research is conducted with few participants and often tested and applicable only in highly controlled environments. However, brain imaging and brain mapping techniques can serve as a bridge that link the digital representation of multimedia and the perception and comprehension of its content. In this thesis I extend the scope of EEG specifically to investigate the perception of visual output from computer graphics applications and create methods based on direct neural feedback for more realistic settings that are applicable for a variety of real-world problems. EEG is a particularly interesting modality for graphics research because it is non-invasive, relatively easy to use, and the cost of equipment is low.

This thesis theorizes that EEG is a viable modality for investigating high-level perceptual problems in graphics. It presents an initial proof-of-concept for the use of EEG for the analysis of human visual perception for graphics problems. To demonstrate this theory I test the following hypotheses :

- Different image and video qualities will evoke a measurable neural response;

- The neural response to different image and video qualities can be classified with a single trial of EEG data;

- Neural responses to varying image and video qualities can be used in a feedback loop to optimize image/video parameters.

1.1. Thesis structure and contribution

Parts of this dissertation have been presented at various peer-reviewed conferences and journals including ACM CHI Conference on Human Factors in

15

Computing System, Transactions on Applied Perception and IEEE Computer Graphics and Applications and have been published in the according conference proceedings [MLM12] and journals [MGM12, MM14]. The basis of this dissertation is founded on these publications but combines them in the unifying concept of creating an interdisciplinary field that integrates brain imaging with computer graphics applications and discusses the opportunities and challenges in this field.

After a short introduction and overview of the necessary background in Chapter 2 I examine the problems in graphics that can be improved by a better understanding of how the human perceptual system works. In Chapter 3 we investigate the perception of different rendering artifacts appearing in videos. My work shows that it is possible to use EEG data to see the distinct differences in the perception of different artifacts occurring in rendered videos and images. Chapter 4 proposes a new methodology to classify single trial EEG data based on the artifact seen by the user. In Chapter 5 we explore the possibility of using a neural feedback loop to optimize image and video parameters to enhance the perception of the videos and images for each individual user.

I conclude in the last part with some thoughts and discussions about the achieved results, draw a conclusion and give an outlook on future work and already published work by others that build on the results of this thesis.

2. Prerequisites

2.1. EEG Basics

EEG measures the electrical activity of a large number of neurons close to the brain surface. Traditional EEG systems require anywhere from 32 to 64 electrodes to be fitted to the head of a participant at specific locations (Fig 2.1). This is usually achieved with a cap of attached electrode positions that is pulled over the head. To ensure conductivity between the electrodes and the scalp, contact gel needs to be applied to the electrodes which is a time-consuming and messy procedure.

Figure 2.1.: Participant performing an EEG experiment

17

Fig. 2.2 shows the electrode placement in the traditional 10-20 electrode system for 32 electrodes. This system is based on the relationship between the location of an electrode and the underlying area of cerebral cortex. Each electrode placement has a letter to identify the lobe and a number to identify the hemisphere location. The letters F, C, P and O are for frontal, central, parietal, and occipital lobes. Even numbers (2,4,6,8) refer to electrode positions on the right hemisphere, while odd numbers (1,3,5,7) refer to those on the left hemisphere. Each scalp electrode is located near certain brain centers, roughly. F7 is located near centers for rational activities, Fz near intentional and motivational centers, F8 close to sources of emotional impulses. Electrode positions C3, C4, and Cz deal with sensory and motor functions. Locations near P3, P4, and Pz contribute to activity of perception and differentiation. Primary visual areas are below locations O1 and O2. However, these are rough estimations and may not reflect the particular areas of cortex accurately, as the exact location of the active sources is still an open problem due to limitations caused by the non-homogeneous properties of the skull and different orientation of the cortex sources.

EEG signals from electrodes must be amplified before they can be converted to digital form and stored. They also need to be filtered to remove artifacts from amplification and sampling. Another type of artifact to be considered and removed originates from eye blinks and facial muscle movements.

Typically, the brain's response to a stimulus is analyzed using event-related potentials (ERP) which measure the response to sudden changes in stimuli. Given that EEG data reflects many concurrent neural processes, the response to

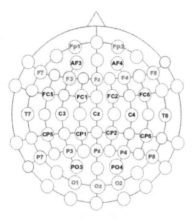

Figure 2.2.: Electrode positions and labels in the 10-20 system with 32-electrodes in a BioSemi cap [bio13]. Each electrode corresponds to a specific underlying brain regions.

a single event is not directly visible in the recording of a single trial, Fig.2.3(a). Many identical trials must be conducted to average out any non-related brain activity in order to make the ERP waveform visible, Fig. 2.3(b). Averaging is done by extracting the segment of EEG surrounding the stimulus from each trial and electrode and lining them up with respect to the start of the stimulus (Fig. 2.3(a)) [Luc05]. An ERP waveform can be time-locked to any externally observable event referenced to the onset of the stimulus. The resulting ERP's consist of positive and negative voltage deflections which allow us to visualize cognitive processing during a trial. In Fig. 2.3(b), the peaks and troughs are labelled P1, N1, P2, N2 and P3. The initial P1 component occurs regardless of the type of stimulus and is just the response to any visual stimulus.

The N1 component is the matching process whenever a stimulus is presented, it is matched with previously experienced stimuli. In contrast, the P3 wave, which occurs approximately 300ms after stimulus onset, depends on the task being performed and the visual stimulus presented [Luc05]. It is hypothesized that the P3 component, which has been a major component of research, reflects the speed of stimulus classification resulting from discrimination of one event from another. Shorter latencies indicate superior mental performance relative to longer latencies. This can be seen from Fig. 2.3(b) which is the response to an oddball experiment where the participants were shown sequences consisting of 80 percent Xs and 20 percent Os and were asked to press one button for X and another for O. Since the frequency of O was much less, the P3 component response is much higher than for X.

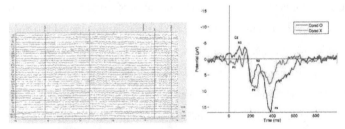

(a) Labelled EEG data over time from a single trial: Each curve corresponds to one electrode.

(b) Averaged curve of many trials for one electrode.

Figure 2.3.: Raw EEG data shows no distinct peaks in response to stimulus occurrence (vertical lines in a). By averaging many identical trials, time-locked to the onset of the stimulus, the Event Related Potential (ERP) becomes visible.

One reason why ERPs have particularly been used for perception and attention research has been the temporal resolution of EEG measurements which allows measuring brain activity from one millisecond to the next. Also given the nature of electrical activity there is no measurable delay between brain activity generated inside the head and the potentials recorded from the scalp. This makes EEG a particularly useful tool for studying time-critical, temporally resolved, real-time brain responses to sensory input.

Recently, researchers have also experimented with using EEG for graphics problems based on ERP measurements [LM11, LWM11]. Unfortunately, the ERP method is time-consuming and it requires many participants and many trials per participant. Recent advances in EEG research have overcome this impediment by creating methods for the analysis and classification of single-trial data [PBSDS06, MGPF99, RMGP00]. In the following, we explore the current work in applying EEG to graphics and the future of EEG as a viable modality for graphics research. To record the EEG data, we use a BioSemi ActiveTwo system [bio13] with 32 electrodes placed on the scalp according to the International 10-20 system. The sampling rate is 256 Hz at 24-bit digitization resolution. In addition, the horizontal and vertical electroocculograms (EOG) and the EEG at both mastoids are recorded. The mastoids were used to remove any data with muscle movements or eye blinks. This setup is used for all the experiments presented in this thesis.

2.2. EEG and Graphics

Until recently, the use of EEG outside specialized fields was restricted not only due to the cost of EEG equipment but also because setting up the apparatus and decoding the signals required considerable technical knowledge. With the advent of technologies like the Emotiv EEG neural headset [Emo12], many of these limitations no longer apply. The headset is cheap, wireless, and gel-less,which makes it much easier to use (However,the signal-to-noise ratio for this system is much lower than for medical-grade EEG devices, and the system has not yet been validated for perceptual research). Also, with the vast amount of research in EEG signal analysis from the BCI and signal processing communities, data analysis has become a less critical issue. EEG is particularly interesting for graphics research because EEG data allows the covert monitoring of reactions to stimuli (images and videos) that might be perceived subconsciously but are consciously ignored (unattended versus attended stimuli) [Mul73]. The greatest advantage of EEG, however, is speed. Complex patterns of neural activity can be recorded occurring within fractions of a second after a stimulus has been presented. For example, while the viewer is watching a video or playing a computer game, the neural response can be recorded simultaneously. This can be an important advantage especially in graphics research, in which the perceptual and emotional response to visual content often plays a major role. While the neural regions responsible for functions such as colour perception, motion detection and orientation in the occipital lobe are relatively well defined, higher-level processes like emotion are more complicated to isolate. Similarly, some event-related potential (ERP) components can be detected even when the subject is not attending to the stimuli. Also, unlike other means of studying reaction time, ERPs can illuminate stages of processing (rather than just the final end result) [SRP98].

EEG has previously been successfully used in BCI research to provide communication and control capacities to people with severe motor disabilities. Brain-machine interfaces have developed at a rapid pace since early experimental demonstrations that used data from simultaneously recorded motor cortex neurons for real-time device control [CMMN99]. Since then BCI's designed for both experimental and clinical studies have been developed that can translate raw neuronal signals into motor commands that reproduce arm reaching and hand grasping movements [LN06]. Typical features of brain activity used include slow cortical potentials, P300 evoked potentials, sensorimotor rhythms recorded from the scalp, event-related potentials recorded on the cortex, and neuronal action potentials recorded within the cortex [SMH+04].

BCI researchers have also explored the possibility of biofeedback-modulated games which respond to neural signals in addition to the traditional mouse or game controller input. For example, researchers at the University College Dublin and Medalab Europe have created a BCI game called the MindGame where neural responses are translated into character movements on a 3D game board [FLR09]. BCI researchers have also been exploring the possibilities of combining neural feedback within a virtual world. Bayliss [Bay03] presents a study where subjects were asked to control several objects within a virtual apartment via EEG. Their studies showed that the EEG data between subjects immersed in a virtual world versus those viewing a monitor did not significantly differ.

One particularly challenging problem in neuroscience has been to decode mental content from brain activity. Functional magnetic resonance imaging (fMRI) have shown that it is, in fact, possible to determine orientation, position and object category from brain activity [HR05, KT05]. Unlike these studies which used simple stimuli Naselaris et al. and Kay et al. [NPK+09, KNPG08] use fMRI data from early and anterior visual areas to reconstruct complex natural images. Given that fMRI's require expensive equipment researchers have also explored the possibility of measuring subconscious cognitive processing using an EEG. Visual category recognition is a difficult problem and usually requires human involvement to label data to allow the system to learn visual categories. Kapoor et al. [KST08] present a framework that combines a discriminative visual category recognition system with EEG data gathered while users view different images. Similarly, Sajda et al. [SPW+10] use an EEG to automatically identify and label interesting images. This research uses EEG to try to understand and utilize the brain's ability to effortlessly recognize and sort objects under extreme variations in scale, lighting, and object shape.

Neuroimaging techniques are particularly interesting from a graphics perspective because our brain can easily accomplish tasks that are problematic for computer algorithms, e.g., edge detection, image categorization or depth estimation. Graphics researchers have over the last many years been interested in the application of visual perception to computer graphics to create realistic imagery.

Realism typically implies computational expense, and knowledge of human visual perception can be used to cut corners and minimize rendering times by guiding algorithms to compute only what is necessary to satisfy the observer. While BCI researchers have expanded the use of EEG and are now studying ways to effectively use neural data for content categorization, virtual reality exploration and immersive gaming experiences [Bay03, FLR09, SYH+07], graphics research so far has not explored the potential of neural feedback for its applications. This thesis expands the scope of graphics research by exploring the use of EEg as a novel modality for graphics problems.

3. Image and Video quality assessment using EEG

3.1. Introduction

In this chapter I hypothesize that different types of rendering artifacts appearing in an image sequence will produce measurable neural responses. Image and video based rendering techniques allow for the creation of realistic 3D scene depictions from only a few images. The ubiquitous use of 3D cinema, affordable display technology, and the merging of real world scenes with computer graphics allows for the creation and pervasive use of realistically rendered images and videos for movies such as Avatar. Similarly, applications like Google Street View use a sparse set of images to create complex visualizations, and Microsoft photosynthesis uses image based rendering to transition between images [SSS06]. However, one of the main areas that still require a lot of research is the assessment and perception of the rendered output. Rendering systems can now closely approximate a real scene, but physical or statistical accuracy does not necessarily amount to visual accuracy. During rendering visually objectionable artifacts can arise which limit the application of most rendering algorithms. The most common artifacts that occur in image-based rendering are ghosting, blurring and popping [VCL$^+$11]. This chapter presents experimental work to analyse the perception and saliency of these artifacts.

While current work in computer vision and graphics focuses on the explicit (overt) output of the human visual system (HVS) in this chapter I propose to use the implicit (covert) processing of the HVS to determine the perception of specific artifacts within a video. There is extensive literature dealing with implicit and explicit processing in the human brain [ST08]. Koch and Tsuchiya [KT07] discuss the evidence showing that visual processing can occur without conscious perception or attention and that conscious awareness of a stimulus is preceded by complex visual decision making processes. This chapter presents the first step in the use of neural responses, recorded with an EEG, to assess the quality of a video with artifacts. In this study I also specifically chose to look at motion in rendered sequences as motion plays an important role in perception owing to effects such as speed and direction of motion, visual tracking of moving objects and motion saliency. Given the complexity of the HVS in perceiving motion, traditional systems based on it have not been able to effectively model temporal aspects of human vision [PLZ$^+$09].

There are several advantages to developing methodologies that merge covert human visual processing with traditional computer graphics and vision techniques. First the analysis of visual information processing that occurs in the absence of conscious attention will allow boosting of traditional masking and rendering algorithms and introduce the robustness and flexibility associated with human vision. Second, such an analysis of the covert visual processes reveals aspects of how these artifacts are viewed by the HVS that have not yet been accurately modelled by computer vision algorithms. Given that it is more important for rendered images and videos to be perceptually accurate as opposed to physically accurate, rendering times can be shortened by eliminating computations that calculate image features that are not apparent to the human eye [MMBH10]. Computer graphics algorithms can take advantage of the limitations of the human eye to compute just enough detail in an image or video to convince the observer without a perceived deterioration in quality.

Here I present the design and results from my experiments with video stimuli containing five different types of artifacts. I present an analysis and comparison of the covert visual decision making about the video quality obtained from the EEG with the conscious video quality judgement obtained via direct user feedback.

3.2. Related work

There has been early interest in studying visual processing for image rendering and analysis techniques [FSPG96]. However, very little work has been done in using implicit visual decision making processes for video assessment. Shenoy et al. [ST08] present the idea of Human-Aided Computing which uses an EEG to label images implicitly. They use brain processes to show that users can implicitly categorize pictures based on content. Their work, however, required users to memorize the images and to be attentive to the content viewed. Our work looks to analyse the implicit visual processing behind viewing videos with motion and not static images. Similarly, Vangorp et al. [VCL$^+$11] conduct psychophysical experiments to understand the perception of artifacts in synthetic renderings. They looked at the user feedback from rendered sequences that moved over facades of buildings. This work focused on the output of conscious visual cognitive processes. Recently Lindemann et al. [LM11, LWM11] have been using an EEG to assess the quality of compressed images and video artifacts. They reported that when shown different images of decreasing quality the participants EEG results showed corresponding detected changes in image quality. Their work showed that the brain response varied with image compression ratio.

3.3. Experiment Procedure

This experiment was designed to measure the covert (implicit) visual processing associated with three basic types of artifacts that typically occur in image based rendering. 8 (3 male, 5 female) healthy participants with an average age of 25 and with normal or corrected-to-normal vision took part in the experiment. All participants had average experience with digital footage and no involvement in professional image/video rendering or editing. The basic stimulus for the experiment was a 5.6 second video (resolution: 1440x1024 pixels, 30 fps) of a person walking along a park trail from left to right. The occurrence of the artifact was delayed by $\pm$ 4 frames ($\pm$ 132ms) to avoid locking the participants attention to a fixed time. Five different kinds of artifacts were incorporated

(a) Ghosting   (b) Blurring

(c) Dashed: area for static blurring and popping, solid:
moving frame for blurring and popping on person

Figure 3.1.: Example of typical rendering artifacts shown in the videos.

into the scene. These artifacts included both temporal and spatial aspects. The following 6 test cases were shown (Fig. 3.1):

1. Popping on person: a small rectangular area (marked with solid line in Fig. 3.1) containing the walking person freezes for one frame

2. Popping: A static rectangular area of the image (marked with dashed line in Fig. 3.1) freezes for one frame.

3. Blurring on person: a small rectangular area containing the walking person is blurred with a Gaussian kernel with a size of 15 pixels in 10 successive frames. The blurring area moves along with the motion of the person

4. Blurring: A static rectangular area (Fig. 3.1) in the center of the scene is blurred with a Gaussian kernel with a size of 15 pixels in 10 successive frames.

5. Ghosting on Person: A partly transparent silhouette of the person stays behind for 10 frames, fading to invisibility in the last 5 frames (left part of Fig. 3.1).

6. Ground truth: No artifacts.

One trial consisted of a ready screen followed by the video with artifacts which was instantly followed by the quality assessment screen. Participants were instructed to follow the moving person with their gaze and rate the quality of every test case on an integer 1 (worst) to 5 (best) mean opinion score (MOS) scale [Int06]. The participants were not informed about the presence of artifacts in the videos.

They were instructed orally and received a training in which every one of the 6 videos was shown 3 times. This prepared for the procedure and showed the whole range of available video qualities. During the main experiment all videos were shown 30 times resulting in 180 trials per participant. The videos

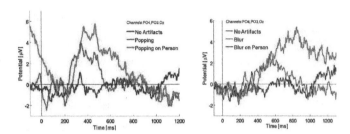

Figure 3.2.: The ERPs for artifacts 'Popping' and 'Popping on person', 'Blurring', 'Blurring on Person' and 'no artifact' averaged over all trials and participants.

were played in a block wise randomized order and the same video was not shown twice in a row.

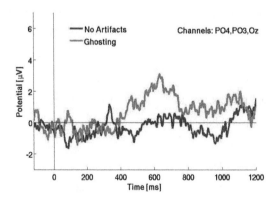

Figure 3.3.: The ERPs for artifacts 'Ghosting' and 'no artifact', averaged over all trials and participants.

An EEG was recorded with 32 electrodes attached according to the international 10-20 system. Additionally a 4 channel EOG and mastoids were recorded which were used as a reference to remove data with accidental eye movements. The recorded data were referenced to the mastoids and filtered with a high-pass filter with a cutoff frequency of 0.1 Hz to remove DC-offset and drift. Trials of a length of 1.2 seconds time locked to the appearance of the artifact occurrence were extracted from the continuous data. All trials with blinks, severe eye movements and too many alpha waves were manually removed.

3.4. Results

Fig. 3.2 and 3.3 show the different ERPs averaged over all participants over all trials and over electrodes PO4, PO3 and Oz. For comparison the 'no artifact' ERP with time 0, corresponding to the appearance of the artifact is included. The validity of the curves was confirmed with a standard two-tailed t-test. The two-tailed t-test tells us the probability that two sets of values come from different groups A. The traditionally accepted P-value for something to be significant is $P < 0.05$. So if there is less than a 5% chance that two sets came from the same group, then it is considered a significant difference between the two sets. In our case for all artifact cases, the two tailed t-test was run for the stimuli time period against the same ground truth time period. In all cases the null hypothesis was rejected and the p-values for 'popping', 'popping on person', 'blurring on person' and 'ghosting' were p<0.0001 while for 'blurring' the p-value was p<0.004. Given the rejection of the null hypothesis in all cases and the fact that the probabilities are all less than 0.05(5%) there is sufficient evidence for the statistical significance of the results. Two-tailed t-test between 'popping' and 'popping on person' and 'blurring' against 'blurring on person' were also computed. Both of these tests also rejected the null hypothesis with p-values of p<0.0001. Given these values we can safely assume a statistically significant difference between the responses over all artifacts. To determine the deviation of individual participants from the average a two-tailed t-test of one randomly selected participant against the averaged results of all the other participants was computed. For all stimuli the null hypothesis was accepted and the p-values were 'popping' p=0.14, 'popping on person' p=0.86, 'blurring'=0.85, 'blurring on person'=0.97 and 'ghosting' p=0.74. Given these p-values and the acceptance of the null hypothesis it is clear that any one participant's response is close to the average. There are no statistically significant differences.

The evaluation of the ERPs provides some very interesting insights. Firstly, all artifacts were detected by the brain, albeit with varying strength. The artifact which evoked the greatest ERP response was 'popping on the moving person' which has a latency of 264ms and reaches a maximum amplitude of 5.758μV. This is followed closely by 'blurring on the moving person'. Static 'popping' and 'blurring' evoke a smaller response. Apparently, 'popping' is a more obviously perceived artifact which evokes an quicker response. Ghosting, however, seems to require the brain to process the perceived distortion before a response occurs. This latency due to processing of the perceived stimuli is also seen with blurring, which is also a less obvious artifact. Table 1 shows the detailed latency and maximum potential responses for all artifacts.

From both the ERP figures and Table 3.1 the second result that becomes clear is the difference in the perception of artifacts related to motion and those independent of motion. Both popping and blurring linked with the motion of the person produce a much larger response potential than popping and blurring not linked with the motion of the person.

Artifacts	Peak Latency (ms)	Peak Amplitude (μV)
Popping on pers.	264	5.758
Popping	200-250	3.928
Blurring on pers.	400	5.58
Blurring	400	2.681
Ghosting	400	3.082

Table 3.1.: Peak latency and amplitude for all artifacts.

Fig. 3.4 shows an average of the participant responses for all trials for each video. As can be seen participants rated the quality of the video with the ghosting artifact as the best after ground truth. This is in contradiction with what the ERPs indicate where although the latency of both blurring and ghosting was the same the ghosting artifact evoked a response with a maximum potential of 3.082μV as opposed to 2.681μV for blurring. The most obvious difference between the explicit quality rating and the implicit brain reaction can be seen between the 'popping on person' and 'popping' artifact. Participants rated the two with almost the same rating (1-1.5) whereas the ERP's show a

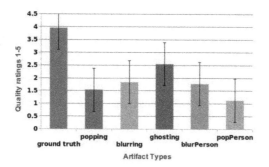

Figure 3.4.: Participants average responses to videos where error bars show variance around mean.

marked difference in the response of the brain to either artifact. This same difference is also observed in the two blurring artifacts. The participants rated them both equally whereas the ERPs show a marked difference between the two (6.58μV and 2.68μV) with the same latency.

3.5. Discussion

These initial experiments provide valuable information about the perception of commonly occurring rendering artifacts. One interesting result is the difference in response to artifacts linked with motion versus artifacts not linked with motion. Artifacts linked with motion seem to evoke a stronger response. Although, motion artifacts occurred on the moving person, whom the participants were instructed to follow, the static artifacts were designed to appear within the center of the participants vision, i.e., the static artifacts did not appear in the periphery.

These results are consistent with findings from perceptual studies that show the HVS to be particularly fine-tuned for the detection of motion in not only the foveal but also in the periphery of vision [MN84]. These experiments can be extended to include additional information about the underlying origins of the neural signals which would provide the exact neural response to a specific property of the stimulus. For example, area V5 of the visual cortex is thought to be responsible for the perception of motion [HBZ89], so a decoupling of the neural response to extract signals originating from V5 would provide valuable information about the motion properties of these artifacts. That analysis is however, beyond the scope of this thesis.

3.6. Summary

These work show that the covert (implicit) and overt (explicit) output of the human visual processing does differ and in some cases the difference is striking. The results show that the brain responds very differently to not only different types of artifacts but also to artifacts specifically linked with motion. This analysis provides information on the perception of videos which has previously not been modelled. This also creates the possibility of shortening rendering times by eliminating computations that calculate image features which do not evoke a strong reaction in the brain as opposed to those which do. The brains response to artifacts is also essential for the modelling of masking algorithms for rendered image sequences.

These first experiments show the possibilities of the use of EEG data for video and image quality assessment. The next chapter presents a method for the single trial classification of artifacts in videos and images.

4. Single Trial Analysis of EEG data

4.1. Introduction

In this chapter I use the data from Chapter 3 to shorten the analysis process of EEG data from multiple trials averaged over multiple participants to a single trial from a single participant. One of the main impediments to the use of an EEG for image quality assessment is the very low Signal-to-Noise Ratio (SNR) which makes it exceedingly difficult to distinguish neural responses from noise. Traditionally, event-related potentials have been used for analysis of EEG data. However, they rely on averaging and so require a large number of participants and trials to get meaningful data. Due the low SNR ERPs are not directly suited for single-trial classification.

In this chapter I propose a novel wavelet-based approach for evaluating EEG signals which allows prediction of perceived image quality from only a single trial. The wavelet-based algorithm is able to filter the EEG data and remove noise, eliminating the need for many participants or many trials. With this approach it is possible to use data from only 10 electrode channels for single-trial classification and predict the presence of an artifact with an accuracy of 85%. We also show that it is possible to differentiate and classify a trial based on the exact type of artifact viewed. Our work is particularly useful for understanding how the human visual system responds to different types of degradations in images and videos. An understanding of the perception of typical image-based rendering artifacts forms the basis for the optimization of rendering and masking algorithms.

4.2. Related Work

Image based rendering (IBR) is a vast area. In this chapter I will only be focusing on the relevant perceptually based algorithms and related work in perceptual IBR. There has been recent interest in studying visual processing for image rendering and analysis techniques [FSPG96, VCL$^+$11]. However, most of the research is geared towards using perception-based algorithms to create rendered sequences [MVL00] or perceptual algorithms that determine the quality of the rendered output [SB10]. Most of the current work with EEG in real world environments has been in the area of Human Computer Interaction (HCI). Wang et al. [WPH$^+$09] present the Brain Computer Interface and Visual Pattern Mining (BCI-VPM) system for rapid image retrieval from an initial subset of images. EEG data is used as input to a pattern mining system to help identify and retrieve relevant images. Their system is an attempt to overcome the manual effort required to annotate a vast library of images for easy access and retrieval.

More relevant is the work of Vangorp et al. [VCL$^+$11] who conduct psychophysical experiments to understand the perception of artifacts in synthetic rendering. They looked at the user feedback from rendered sequences that panned over facades of buildings. I use their work to decide the kind of artifacts to look into. This work is focused on using an EEG to measure the actual perception of these artifacts in the primary visual cortex and to then use these measurements to determine the overall perceptual quality of the videos. We also choose to look at complicated videos to determine how the HVS responds to complex photorealistic images as opposed to simplistic synthetic visual stimuli.

4.2.1. Perception Based Rendering Algorithms

In 2001, McNamara [McN01] investigated the idea of including a perceptual model into the rendering pipeline. She presents perceptual algorithms which focus on embedding models of the HVS directly into global illumination computations in order to improve their efficiency. However, she mentions that perception overall is a much more complex process that requires more research in the future.

In the same year, Luebcke and Hallen [LH01] used an approximation to an empirical perceptual model for real-time rendering. They used a point-based rendering system called QSplat [RL00] that constructed a point-cloud hierarchy over a given model. The point cloud was then used during rendering as a multi-resolution approximation of the underlying geometry. The perceptual model was combined with gaze tracking to produce a detailed map that defined the required rendering precision.

As a conservative estimation of the perceptual quality, Farrugia and Péroche [FP04] use information from the human visual system, to define when an approximated image is indistinguishable from its original. Even though their approximated images are perceptually of the same quality, they miss out on further optimizations due to the remaining perceptual processing.

As part of a 2010 Siggraph Course by Křivánek et.al [KFC$^+$10] on ray-tracing solutions for film production rendering, Fajardo gave an example of a case where all prior metrics would fail to some extent. In order to reduce the noise in indirect illumination, all specular lobes are widened in secondary bounces. This leads to a convincing looking image without any visual artifacts that accurately conveys the overall lighting situation. However, it is very well distinguishable compared against a ground truth reference.

4.2.2. Wavelet-Based Analysis

In recent years, wavelet-based and especially shift-invariant (aka. complex) wavelet-based analysis has become more popular in the context of EEG or brain wave data. However, most of the publication in these areas are either focusing on strong abnormalities or more invasive brain wave recording than EEG [SAKK05].

Olkkonen et al. [OPOZ06] were the first ones to apply a complex wavelet transform for filtering EEG data. They used a separate Hilbert transform in

Fourier space, therefore guaranteeing true shift-invariance. In order to avoid the required Fourier transformations the authors also proposed to use a discrete version of the Hilbert transform as defined by Oppenheim et.al [OSB99].

With the advent of lifting steps to create second generation wavelets [SS00], a different construction of the complex wavelet transform can be implemented. Barria et al. [BDS12] show that the resulting dual-tree wavelet transformation almost form a Hilbert pair. Since we would like to achieve the highest classification accuracy rather than optimal running time, we chose to stay with the separate Hilbert transform and the lifting algorithm for final transform only. The complex wavelet transform and its application to EEG data is further explained in the following sections.

All final classifications require some kind of either support vector machine (SVM) or neural network. As SVMs are very well established in this field, we chose a multi-class support vector machine (C-SVM) with radial basis functions (RBF) as the kernel function. The SMV we use throughout this paper is freely available from the authors [CL11].

4.3. Artifact Classification

The most straightforward way to classify single-trial EEG data is using it in its raw form. While this is useful for ERPs where a large number of trials are averaged, the low signal-to-noise ratio and the overall amount of noise makes this approach unsuitable for the single trial setting.

Traditionally, the variants of the discrete Fourier transform have been used as the brain activity is limited to certain frequency ranges and most of the frequencies outside of these ranges can be regarded as noise [MLHB92]. However, since the Fourier transform loses all temporal information outside a single phase shift per frequency, it cannot be used directly. The main difference is that wavelets are localized in both time and frequency whereas the standard Fourier transform is only localized in frequency.

In contrast to the discrete Fourier transform, the discrete wavelet transform (DWT) has a much lower frequency resolution but temporal resolution varies with the frequency, i.e. the temporal resolution is directly proportional to the frequency. Since each frequency range we're interested in roughly covers one frequency band of the wavelet transform, it seems to be the ideal choice for us. However, a regular wavelet transform is not shift invariant and will therefore have issues with phase shifts. A complex discrete wavelet transform (CDWT), on the other hand, can easily be made shift invariant as we will see below.

When analysing EEG data from face and object recognition, Rousselet et.al. [RHBS07] found that the 5Hz to 15Hz range produced the best results in their setting. However, initial experiments showed that using the range from 2.5Hz to 20Hz increases the classification accuracy compared to 5Hz to 20Hz (we can't use 5Hz to 15Hz as we are limited to multiples of 2 because of the wavelet transform). This can be explained by the slightly less than perfect frequency cut-off of the wavelet filter functions (see Fig. 4.2) and the fact that a lower frequency phase shift shows up in higher frequency bands.

4.3.1. Wavelet Transformation

Given a discrete input signal $f(t)$ and the wavelet filter pair consisting of a low-pass filter $g(t)$ and a high-pass filter $h(t)$, the general discrete wavelet transform is defined as follows:

$$s_0(t) = f(t)$$
$$s_{n+1}(t) = \sum_{k=-\infty}^{\infty} s_n(k) g(2t-k)$$
$$d_{n+1}(t) = \sum_{k=-\infty}^{\infty} s_n(k) h(2t-k)$$

In case of the Haar wavelet [Haa10], functions g and h form a orthonormal basis and are defined as follows:

$$g(t) = \begin{cases} 1 & 0 \leq t \leq 2 \\ 0 & \text{otherwise} \end{cases}$$

$$h(t) = \begin{cases} 1 & 0 \leq t \leq 1 \\ -1 & 1 \leq t \leq 2 \\ 0 & \text{otherwise} \end{cases}$$

In turn, this leads to the very simple definition of the Haar transform:

$$s_0(t) = f(t)$$

$$
\begin{aligned}
d_{n+1}(t) &= s_n(2t+1) - s_n(2t) \\
s_{n+1}(t) &= \frac{1}{2}s_n(2t) + \frac{1}{2}s_n(2t+1)
\end{aligned}
$$

As can be seen, s_n is simply the average of two consecutive samples and d_n is the delta between these two. In order to easily construct higher order wavelets, we use an approach called lifting [SS00] where the calculation of s_{n+1} is based on d_{n+1} as well. The Haar wavelet transform can then be written as follows:

$$
\begin{aligned}
d_{n+1}(t) &= s_n(2t+1) - s_n(2t) \\
s_{n+1}(t) &= s_n(2t) + \frac{1}{2}d_{n+1}(t)
\end{aligned}
$$

Since we are interested in frequency ranges however, we need to take a closer look at the frequency response of the Haar wavelet filter pair. As seen in Fig. 4.1, for the Haar wavelet there is both a large frequency overlap between the wavelet and the scaling function. Furthermore, there are a significant amount of frequencies outside of the optimal ranges that will show up in the frequency bands.

In order to get both a better frequency cut-off and less overlap between wavelet and scaling function, higher order wavelets, such as cubic B-spline wavelets (see Fig. 4.2) can be used. Note that the cut-off frequencies can be different for each wavelet but they always follow the rule that the frequency doubles from one band to the next.

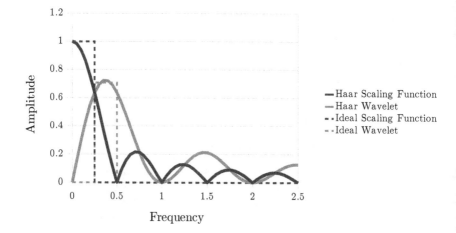

Figure 4.1.: Frequency response of Haar wavelet and scaling function compared against optimal frequency cut-off.

The lifting steps for the cubic B-spline wavelet transform are as follows:

$$
\begin{aligned}
d_{n+1}(t) &= s_n(2t+1) \\
&\quad -\frac{9}{16}s_n(2t+2) + \frac{1}{16}s_n(2t+4) \\
&\quad -\frac{9}{16}s_n(2t) + \frac{1}{16}s_n(2t-2) \\
s_{n+1}(t) &= s_n(2t) \\
&\quad +\frac{9}{32}d_{n+1}(t) - \frac{1}{32}d_{n+1}(t+1)
\end{aligned}
$$

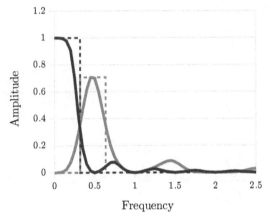

Figure 4.2.: Frequency response of cubic B-spline wavelet and scaling function compared against optimal frequency cut-off.

$$+\frac{9}{32}d_{n+1}\left(t-1\right)-\frac{1}{32}d_{n+1}\left(t-2\right)$$

Unfortunately, the wavelet transform is not shift invariant due to its down-sampling property, i.e. the fact the each set of samples d_{n+1} contains only half the number of samples as d_n. However, the family of B-spline wavelets, as any discrete, symmetric filter, is linear in the phase of incoming frequencies which means that the filter has no phase distortion or constant group delay.

4.3.2. Shift Invariant Transform

In order to create a shift invariant wavelet transform, we either have to make our input signal or the actual transform shift invariant in some sense. However, the easiest way to create a shift invariant transform is making the input shift invariant using an analytic function.

Analytic Function

The analytic function is defined as a complex function where the imaginary part is the same as the real, except that all frequencies have been shifted by 90 degree. Since the 90 degree shift is also linear in phase, the transformation from real to imaginary has constant group delay. The analytic function is defined using the Hilbert transform H as follows:

$$f_a(t) \quad = \quad f(t) + jH(f)(t)$$

If we assume that f^* consists of a single frequency, we get:

$$f^*(t) \quad = \quad a\sin(\omega t + x)$$
$$f_a^*(t) \quad = \quad a(\sin(\omega t + x) + j\cos(\omega t + x))$$

Which leads us to the following for the absolute value of the analytic function of a single frequency:

$$\|f_a^*(t)\| = \|a\| \sqrt{\sin^2(\omega t + x) + \cos^2(\omega t + x)}$$
$$= \|a\|$$

Since the wavelet transform has a linear phase, transforming the function f^* will only change it's amplitude a, the frequency ω and the phase x to a', ω' and x'. Furthermore, applying the wavelet transform on top of the Hilbert transform will produce the exact same result for a', ω' and x'. As the absolute value of the transformed function is now a' regardless of the initial phase, the whole transform is shift invariant.

Hilbert Transformation

So far, we have treated the Hilbert transform as a black-box that causes a phase delay of 90 degrees. There are several ways to write down the Hilbert transform but one of it's continuous closed forms is as follows:

$$H(u)(t) = -\frac{1}{\pi} \lim_{\varepsilon \downarrow 0} \int_\varepsilon^\infty \frac{u(t+\tau) - u(t-\tau)}{\tau} \, d\tau$$

In frequency space, the Hilbert transform is a phase shift by 90 (or $\frac{\pi}{2}$) degree. However, we seek to use a discrete Hilbert transform that does not require a Fourier transform of the EEG data. As the convolution is defined for continuous signals only, we first have to either reconstruct a continuous function from the EEG sample points or calculate discrete filter coefficients using some kind of weighted numeric integration. Since reconstructing a continous EEG signal might introduce unwanted frequencies, we use the discrete Hilbert transformation defined as follows:

$$H_{discrete}(u)(t) \quad = \quad \frac{1}{2\pi} \sum_{\tau} \frac{u(t+\tau)}{\tau - \frac{1}{2}} + \frac{u(t+\tau)}{\tau + \frac{1}{2}}$$

Calculating a discrete Fourier transform on the above kernel shows that this is indeed the exact transform we require.

Complex Wavelet Transformation

Computing a separate Hilbert transformation prior to the actual wavelet transformation as in [OPOZ06] allows us to use the same filter coefficients for both the real and the imaginary filters. At the same time, this approach fits our analysis framework best as it guarantees true shift-invariance (within the limits of the accuracy of the Hilbert transform).

In order to achieve a better frequency cut-off than Olkkonen et.al, we use cubic interpolating spline wavelets with lifting [SS00] for both the real and imaginary portion of our analytic function as this produced the overall highest classification accuracy.

Assuming all input and output coefficients s_i, d_i to be complex numbers, the filter coefficients for the complex wavelet transform are equivalent to the filter coefficients of the regular wavelet transform. Thus, the lifting steps are the same as well.

4.3.3. Support Vector Machine Classification

Before applying the SVM, we remove any data outside the 2.5Hz-5Hz, 5Hz-10Hz and 10Hz-20Hz frequency bands as early experiments and analysis showed that additional frequency bands lead the SVM astray.

We are using a standard support vector machine [CL11] for all classification tasks. For the statistics, we performed a standard 5-fold cross-correlation test.The data is split randomly into 5 groups of 288 trials. Using a C-SVM with a radial basis function (RBF) $e^{-g|x_i - x_j|^2}$ classifier and a set of fixed parameters, the support vector machine is trained with data from 4 groups (976 trials) and tested against the trials in the remaining group (288 trials). This process is repeated until all trials have been classified. As proposed by Chang and Lin [CL11], the process is repeated until the best set of parameters has been found. The 5-fold cross correlation test is implemented as follows:

1. Split input data into 5 groups

2. Exhaustively search for all parameter values of the SVM and basis function

    2.1. For each of the 5 part

        2.1.1. Train the SVM with the 4 other ones

        2.1.2. Test with the selected part

        2.1.3. Record the average success for all parts

    2.2. If the average score was better than for all previously tested parameters remember these

3. Train the SVM with all of the original data and the best set of parameters
   found in 2.2

4.4. Experiment

The experiment follows the same procedure and set up as described in Chapter 3. 8 (3 male, 5 female) healthy participants with an average age of 25 and
with normal or corrected-to-normal vision took part in the experiment. All
participants had average experience with digital footage and no involvement in
professional image/video rendering or editing. Since I already know from earlier experiments that the neural response to the following artifacts is distinct, the
same artifacts are used again, but now for the single trial classification (Fig.3.1):
Popping on Person (popP), Popping, Blurring on person, Blurring, Ghosting
and Ground Truth (GT).

4.5. Results

Fig. 4.4 show relative power increase over time for all artifacts averaged over
all participants over all trials and over electrodes PO4, PO3,Oz, O1 and O2
(Fig 4.3) and as compared with ground truth (gt) with time 0 corresponding
to the appearance of the artifact. We averaged over these electrodes as they
correspond to the primary visual cortex in the brain and the areas that deal with
motion. The EEG signal responding to the visual stimuli is strongest here.

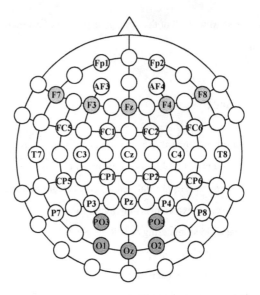

Figure 4.3.: Frontal (F7, F3, Fz, F4 and F8), Occipital (O1, Oz and O2) and Posterior (PO3, PO4) electrode positions used for analysis in this chapter. F3/F7 are in the left frontal cortex and F4/F8 in the right. Fz is in the mid-line region.

All artifacts were detected by the brain. The artifact which evoked the greatest response was 'Popping on Person'(popP) which has the highest relative power and the least latency of response. This is followed closely by popping. 'Popping' is a more obviously perceived artifact and evokes a quicker and stronger response in comparison to 'popping' not linked to motion. Ghosting, as can be seen, has the least response in terms or latency and relative power. It apparently requires the brain to process the perceived distortion before an

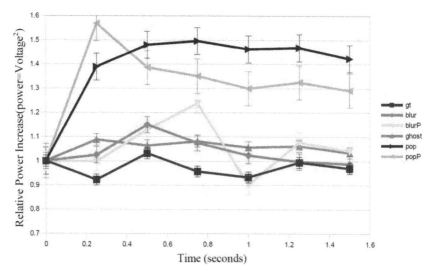

Figure 4.4.: Power increase for all artifacts in the 10Hz - 20Hz range compared against ground truth(gt) where 0 is appearance of artifact and error bars show standard error around mean. The maximum neural response is for the artifacts 'popping' and 'popping on person'.

EEG response is measurable. This latency due to processing of the perceived stimuli is also seen with blurring, which is also a less obvious artifact. However it is interesting to note that blurring linked to motion has a longer latency but a much higher response in terms of relative power increase. From the figures the difference in perception of artifacts related to motion as opposed to those independent of motion is clear. Artifacts linked with motion('popping on person' and 'blurring on person') produce a much larger response than their counterparts ('popping' and 'blurring'),i.e. 'popping on person' evokes a stronger response than 'popping' and similarly 'blurring' on person evokes a stronger response than 'blurring'. The results shown in these plots differ from the ERP's from Chapter 3 since these show the average power increase within a specific frequency (10-20Hz) as opposed to the responses over all frequencies.

4.5.1. Response from Frontal Electrodes

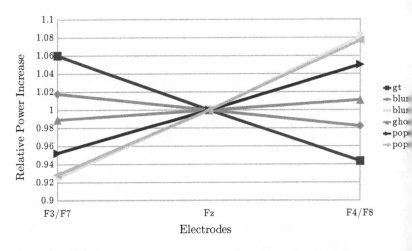

Figure 4.5.: Front electrode response to artifacts in the 10Hz - 20Hz range. F3/F7(averaged) are left frontal cotex and F4/F8(averaged) are right frontal cortex.

As can be seen from Fig. 4.5, apart from a visual response there is a distinct response from the frontal electrodes to the artifacts as well. Previous data from EEG studies and emotion has provided some evidence of lateralization of emotion in the frontal cortex [CA04, ST01, TDH90]. This theory predicts right hemisphere dominance for negative emotions. Fig. 4.5 shows the response from electrodes F3/F7 (averaged), Fz and F4 /F8(averaged). As can be seen from Fig. 4.3 these electrodes are located in the front of the head corresponding to the frontal cortex (yellow electrodes). F3/F7 are in the left frontal cortex and F4/F8 in the right. Fz is in the mid-line region. The results as can be seen from Fig. 4.5 show an increased output in the right frontal cortex for test cases with more severe artifacts where the maximum output was for 'popping on person' and 'blurring on person'. This supports our conclusion that artifacts linked with motion not only evoke a larger visual response but are also emotionally more disturbing. This can theoretically be explained by the negative emotions elicited by bad video quality. It is also interesting to note that there is a difference in the response of these artifacts from the frontal electrodes as compared to the back electrodes. Specifically, 'blurring on person' moves up and has the strongest response with 'popping on person'. Similarly, 'ghosting' also moves above 'blurring'. Ground truth where there were no artifacts seems to evoke a positive emotional response as opposed to the negative responses from the videos with artifacts. However, emotion is a complex process and we can only theorize as to the origins of this asymmetry and difference in response as compared to perceptual areas, seen in our data. Given that the underlying brain regions are responsible for many functions, including decision, making it is possible the response we see is a mix of many different neural processes. Regardless, for the purpose of our classification it is sufficient that the response is predictable and different for each artifact.

4.5.2. Wavelet Based Classification

Given the statistical significance between ground truth and a given artifact in the EEG data [MLM12], we were able to look at a total of three different classification tasks. The three classification categories we look at are:

- We classify trials into one of two categories, trials with artifacts vs trials without artifacts.

- We classify trials based on the severity of the artifact and look to only detect severe artifact, i.e. 'popping' and 'popping on person'.

- We classify each trial based on the specific type of artifact. What artifact does a given trial contain?

We start by looking into only the response from the visual cortex and classifying trials based on that. However, it is interesting to note that as soon as we add the channels used for the emotional analysis, the accuracy of classification improves measurably.

Ground-Truth Classification

Classifying the trials based on if there is an artifact present at all gives us an accuracy of 63% for using only the raw data. Using the wavelet transformed

	Trial Classified as	
Artifact	Ground Truth	Any Artifact
Ground Truth	**75%**	25%
Any Artifact	15%	**85%**

Table 4.1.: Single trial classification accuracy using visual processing and emotional data for ground truth with correct classifications on the diagonal.

visual data increases the accuracy to 71%. Additionally using the wavelet-transformed data from the frontal electrodes further increases the accuracy to 85% (Table 4.1). So for any given single trial from any given participant, we can determine whether an artifact was perceived or not with an accuracy of 85%. This allows us to determine the exact perceived quality of a visual stimulus. It is important to note that we train a SVM with just these two classes rather than using the same as for the per-artifact detection. As we use a differently trained SVM, we actually achieve a better accuracy for classifying ground truth trials at the cost of classifying artifact trials.

Severe Artifact Detection

	Trial Classified as	
Artifact	Ground Truth	Severe Artifact
Ground Truth	**95%**	5%
Severe Artifact	7%	**93%**

Table 4.2.: Single trial classification accuracy using visual processing and emotional data for severe artifacts (popping and popping on person) with correct classifications on the diagonal.

Instead of trying to classify for ground truth, we can also try to find the most severe or objectionable artifacts. Starting with the raw data, we get an accuracy of already 75% (Table 4.1). However, just using the wavelet transformed visual data increases the accuracy to 83%. Again, adding the wavelet transformed frontal electrode data, we get a final accuracy of 93% (Table 4.2), leading us to the conclusion that severe artifacts can be reliably detected the easiest. Therefore with any single trial from any participant we can with an accuracy of 93% determine whether there was a severely perceived distortion in the rendered output. Note that this result was also gained by using a SVM that was trained for specifically recognizing severe artifacts rather than trying to distinguish between artifacts.

Specific Artifact Classification

We also looked into classifying trials based on the exact type of artifact appearing in the videos. Picking a random class for each trial would result in an expected accuracy of 16% so any resulting accuracy needs to be substantially better than this in order to claim successful classification. Feeding all of the raw EEG curves into the SVM results in a classification accuracy of 39%. Using the wavelet transformed visual data only, we get a classification accuracy of 51% (Table 4.3). As can be seen from Table 4.3, 'Popping on Person' is the easiest artifact to classify and 'Ghosting' the hardest. This is in keeping with the way these artifacts are perceived by the HVS, as can also be seen from Fig. 4.4.

Artifact	Trial Classified as					
	Ground Truth	Blurring	Blurring on P.	Ghosting	Popping	Popping on P.
Ground Truth	**50%**	15%	15%	12%	4%	4%
Blurring	10%	**54%**	15%	13%	3%	5%
Blurring on Person	8%	12%	**49%**	17%	5%	9%
Ghosting	17%	17%	18%	**35%**	6%	7%
Popping	7%	6%	4%	5%	**59%**	19%
Popping on Person	5%	5%	8%	4%	16%	**62%**

Table 4.3.: Single trial classification accuracy using data from back electrodes (PO3, O1, Oz, O2, PO4) only on a per-artifact basis with correct classifications on the diagonal.

Finally, using the wavelet transformed frontal electrode data as well, we have a classification accuracy of 64% (Table 4.4). As can be seen from Table 4.4 we can now determine exactly which kind of artifact appeared in any given visual stimulus. So for any given single trial from any one participant we can determine the exact kind of artifact that was perceived by the viewer. As expected, classifying the ghosting artifacts is the worst scenario (but still almost three times as good as random) whereas classifying the 'Popping on Person' is the best one (with 70% accuracy). This allows us to not only determine the perceived quality of a rendered output but also determine the problems with the how it was perceived.

4.6. Discussion

While the current experimental set-up provides new and relevant information it has some limitations. One limitation is that so far this has only been tested with emotionally neutral content. Because of this, a low-grade artifact appearing

Artifact	Trial Classified as					
	Ground Truth	Blurring	Blurring on P.	Ghosting	Popping	Popping on P.
Ground Truth	**63%**	10%	13%	11%	2%	1%
Blurring	11%	**68%**	13%	7%	0%	1%
Blurring on Person	9%	13%	**66%**	8%	1%	3%
Ghosting	17%	12%	18%	**49%**	2%	2%
Popping	3%	2%	3%	5%	**70%**	17%
Popping on Person	3%	2%	4%	2%	19%	**70%**

Table 4.4.: Single trial classification accuracy using data from back electrodes (PO3, O1, Oz, O2, PO4) and front electrodes (F7, F3, Fz, F4, and F8) on a per-artifact basis with correct classifications on the diagonal.

in a highly negative emotional scene might, according to our speculation, be confused with a severe artifact. One way around this is to de-construct the neural response based on the specific underlying brain regions and functionality. This will enable the decoupling of the response to an artifact from emotional response to content. Similarly, so far this technique has only been used for classifying artifacts in a controlled environment so for each artifact the underlying scene was the same. Hypothetically, then, a blurring or ghosting artifact in an empty scene when compared with a popping-linked-with-motion artifact in a busy, cluttered scene, might show a stronger neural response. However, although this might be true, given that our aim is to reduce computational time for rendering algorithms based on how clearly an artifact is perceived, in the above scenario more computational time would then be spent on perfecting an empty, less cluttered scene than a busy cluttered scene.

Another issue is the absence of eye movement information for more complicated test scenes. For our current video we could assume all participants

were following the moving person since there was only one type of movement in the video. We also assumed that the response to motion artifacts was
based on the inherent properties of how the visual system perceives motion
and not on the positioning of the motion versus non-motion artifacts. This
assumption could be made because the experiment was designed to ensure all
artifacts appeared withitn the central ($5°$), paracentral ($8°$) or macular ($18°$)
field of vision. However, this becomes a problem with more complicated test
scenes and for that we need to use an eye tracker. This would allow us to
incorporate information regarding the exact viewing pattern of the participants
during stimuli presentation. A more complete picture of participants' eye gaze
pattern during stimuli presentation is essential for advances in realistic image
and video synthesis. Also, using sensors to capture physiological data would
provide more concrete information regarding the participants' emotional state
during trials.

4.7. Summary

This work introduces a new method for the single trial classification of typical
IBR artifacts. I show that wavelets are an effective way to deal with the problem
of low signal-to-noise ratios inherent in EEG signals. We also show that it is
possible, with a good degree of accuracy to distinguish between different types
of artifacts appearing in video stimuli. This work analyses the way the brain
responds to not only different types of artifacts but also to artifacts specifically
linked with motion. Artifacts linked with motion evoke a much larger response

in the brain. The results presented here also show that there is an emotional component to the neural response to artifacts. Results of this work open up the possibility of exploring the emotional response to not just artifacts but content of rendered image sequences. For example, would it be possible to use an EEG to determine the uncanny valley response to rendered humans? Similarly, EEG data could potentially be used to research the level of immersion of users in virtual environments and propose new methods to improve the interactivity within such environments.

5. The Human in the Loop : EEG-driven Rendering Parameter Optimization

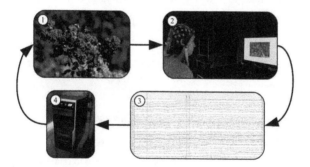

Figure 5.1.: This chapter describes a novel approach to optimize rendering quality based on users' neural response as captured by EEG. Our optimization loop consists of the rendering algorithm whose parameter settings are to be optimized (1), a user who watches the rendering results on screen (2), a pre-trained classifier that analyses the measured EEG response (3), and an optimizer that automatically updates rendering parameter values (4).

5.1. Introduction

Given that EEG is a promising approach for neural feedback in BCI [LGM13], I investigate a novel method to aesthetically enhance videos and images based on a person's perceptual and emotional response, as measured by EEG. The idea is to explore the possibilities of more interactive uses of EEG as direct input to rendering algorithms. Our example application represents a particularly challenging problem since perceived image quality is not always an objective measure. While up to a point, people can largely agree on what distinguishes a higher-quality rendering from a lower-quality image, when it comes to visual aesthetics, there exists considerable diversity of people's personal taste. What's worse, when asked to explain our visual preferences, we typically find it exceedingly difficult to reflect on our aesthetic predilections, or to find objective reasons for their justification.

I investigate the hypothesis that both general visual quality as well as individual preferences can, up to a point, be reliably and reproducibly assessed based on EEG recordings. I record a person's brain response to rendered images and, based on a previously trained Support Vector Machine (SVM), immediately determine from the EEG signal a "visual appeal" score. The score is used to drive a numerical optimization routine that varies the parameter values of the rendering algorithm, changing in turn the rendered image observed by the user. This optimization loop drives the rendered output towards an aesthetic optimum, as perceived by the individual user.

For the purpose of this work we use the term 'quality' to refer to noise or artifacts and 'aesthetics' to denote the 'look' or atmosphere of an image. To evaluate our approach, we consider two different application scenarios. In the first scenario, static photos of real-world scenes are EEG-optimized with respect to saturation, brightness, and contrast according to individual taste. In the second scenario, three rendering parameters are varied to optimize the general appeal of an animation sequence.

5.2. Related Work

5.2.1. Perceptual graphics

Over the last decade, visual perception aspects have entered into computer graphics research. By taking into account how our HVS processes image information, superior rendering and modelling algorithms can be designed [MMBH10]. Perceptual feedback has also been used in the creation of facial composite systems for police work. EvoFit, for example, is a system where witnesses are shown faces with random characteristics and based on witness feedback, certain parameters are optimized and through a process of selection a composite face evolves [FHC04]. This is similar to the approach this chapter presents using feedback from an EEG to optimize parameters.

While this work is also centred on the HVS, I do not present a specific, HVS-adapted algorithm but a general approach to optimize visual output quality applicable for a wide range of rendering algorithms.

5.2.2. Visual quality metrics

For human observers, rating image quality without having a reference, 'ground-truth' image available is a straight-forward exercise. In contrast, it has proven exceedingly difficult to algorithmically define a no-reference visual quality metric that mimics the HVS's perception of visual quality [WB06]. This is especially true for most rendered output as often-times a reference, 'ground-truth' image or video is not available. Recently, a promising no-reference image quality assessment algorithm for realistic rendering has been proposed [HČA$^+$12]. This approached is based on exploiting information about the underlying synthetic scene (e.g., 3D surfaces, textures) instead of merely considering colour, and training the learning framework with typical rendering artifacts. Although this model is useful in detecting rendering artifacts, it does not determine overall perceptual quality of a rendered output. In contrast, my approach circumvents algorithmically assessing visual quality altogether and aims to determine the overall perceptual quality of an image or video based on the EEG response.

5.2.3. Non-photorealistic rendering

The premier goal of Non-Photorealistic Rendering (NPR) is the creation of expressive visual representations [GG01], e.g., for illustration and artistic purposes [SH06, CGL$^+$08]. Evaluating NPR methods involves going beyond mere visual quality and includes also aesthetic aspects [INC$^+$06, Her10]. The approach presented in this chapter may offer a new way to assess NPR algorithms' performance in terms of visual and aesthetic appeal.

5.2.4. EEG in BCI

EEG has been in use for many years in the area of Brain Computer Interfaces (BCI). The focus in BCI is predominantly on controlling devices by consciously altering EEG signals, typically of the sensorimotor area of the brain [ABM08]. Our approach, in contrast, does not require deliberately evoked neural responses but considers EEG data originating from implicit HVS processes in response to an image or video.

5.2.5. EEG and emotion

There is a considerable amount of research that has shown EEG to be a reliable means for determining the emotional state of a user during the performance of various tasks [Bos06, HDR08, CKGP06, MRN+08]. Psychophysiological studies have shown a bilateralization of emotion in the frontal cortex. Left frontal inactivation is an indicator of a withdrawal response, linked to negative emotion while right frontal inactivation is a sign of a positive reaction. We use this as a basis for classifying a positive or negative reaction to an image or video [CA04].

5.2.6. EEG in visual perception

In perceptual psychology, a plethora of research exists on the use of EEG measurements to determine attention and image quality [CA04, N⁺02]. With respect to perceived image quality, recent research suggests that artifacts in compressed images and video can be assessed by detecting Event-related Potentials (ERP) in EEG data [LM11]. ERP detection has also been shown to be able to distinguish between different types of artifacts in video sequences [MLM12, MGM12]. A sudden change in video quality has also been found to elicit a measurable response in the P3 component of EEG data [SBT⁺12]. EEG has also been used to measure the cognitive load when performing a specific task using different visualization techniques [APM⁺11]. The work presented in this chapter extends the range of EEG applications in visual perception and graphics by not relying on sudden visual changes (event). My approach is able to quantify overall visual appeal and individual preference without having to resort to comparison to a reference.

5.2.7. Rendering parameter optimization

Different approaches have been proposed to determine parameter values for various computer graphics algorithms [CCV03]. Techniques based on user feedback include Interactive Evolution [Sim91], Inverse Design [SDS⁺93, KPC93], and Design Galleries [MAB⁺97]. A recent example for automatic lighting parameter optimization was proposed by Shacked et al. [SL01]. A considerable amount of work has also been done in the area of automatic image enhancement [KLW12, HKK12]. Commercial applications like Microsoft's Office Picture Manager, Adobe's Lightroom, and Adobe Photoshop also feature tools for the enhancement of photographs.

Related to my optimization approach is the work of Bychkovsky et al. [BPCD11]. In their work, a database of 5 sets of 5000 photos was adjusted by professional photographers. The result was used for supervised machine learning, focusing on global tonal adjustments. Once trained, the system is able to learn an individual's preference for future adjustments from a small set of images retouched by the user. I make use of the same dataset, and my approach also makes use of supervised learning, albeit of user EEG recordings. In contrast to Bychkovsky et al. [BPCD11], however, my method does not require each new user to go through the effort of retouching a number of photos first. The rationale behind my approach is to use EEG to quantify the notion of visual appeal and that emotional sense of "liking" or "loving" a particular rendition of a picture, a feeling that often times we are unable to translate into objective image properties.

5.3. EEG Optimization Loop

Fig. 5.2 shows the main components of the EEG-driven optimization loop. There is a one-time training phase required to teach the classifier the difference between the neural response to good versus bad visual stimuli. The training phase is conducted with one set of participants who are not part of the testing/optimization phase. Once the classifier is trained, it can optimize a visual

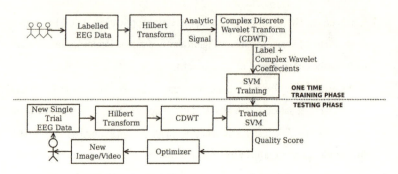

Figure 5.2.: The framework for the optimization loop requires a training phase, which is conducted only once and with a disjoint set of people who are not part of the testing. Afterwards the loop will optimize any video or image for any individual.

stimulus independent of content with a single EEG trial within a loop. The user sees an image or a video, and their EEG is recorded and sent to the Support Vector Machine (SVM)-based classifier. The classifier calculates a score from the EEG data reflecting the user's 'liking' for the image or video. The optimizer, in turn, varies a pre-defined number of parameters of the rendering algorithm in response to the score. The rendering algorithm then re-renders the image or video corresponding to the new parameter values, which is again displayed to the user.

The optimization framework is applicable to any rendering algorithm that generates still images or animated sequences and whose output varies depending on some set of parameter values. The modular set-up allows for easy replacement of the rendering component to optimize different parameters. To evaluate the approach, we present results for two different rendering application scenarios in Section 5.4.

5.3.1. Classifier

Once the classifier has been trained it produces a score value reflecting the visual appeal of the image or video based on the EEG data. However, the raw EEG data has to be preprocessed in several steps before we can extract meaningful information from it [MGM12]. From the continuous raw EEG data we need to select the relevant chunks corresponding to image or video responses followed by a complex wavelet transform to split the input into distinct frequency bands as explained in Section 4.3.1. Finally, we determine the frequencies to use for classification and send the corresponding wavelet coefficients to the SVM in order to produce the score value for the input data.

Data Selection

Depending on the application, we are either interested in the response to a single short event, i.e. new image, or several events in a given time-frame, i.e. short video clip. Since the largest response to an event usually occurs roughly half a second after the actual event and lasts for about one second, we need to analyse the EEG data corresponding to this second. Given multiple events or an unknown event-time we would need to look at any one second time-frame. With a sampling rate of 256Hz, this would be 256 time-frames per second of video. However, we found, based on trial experiments, that looking at time-frames starting every quarter of a second is a good compromise between the amount of data that needs processing and the accuracy of the final classification.

SVM Input

As explained in Chapter 4 we are interested in the overall power for each frequency band over time. We therefore use the absolute value of the complex wavelet coefficients as input to the SVM rather than the complex numbers. Also, we limit the data to the 8Hz to 32Hz range where waking neural activity occurs. We also use data from only a total of eight electrodes. Since we are interested in the visual and emotional response to an image or video, we take the front electrodes (F3 ,Fz and F4) as they are located over the pre-frontal cortex which plays a crucial role in emotion regulation and conscious experience [Bos06]. We also take the back electrodes (PO3,PO4,O1,O2,Oz) as they correspond to the primary visual cortex in the brain and the areas that deal with motion. Altogether, we send a total of 384 wavelet coefficients to the SVM for classification.

Score Generation

During training, a set of possible score values were defined for each training input sample, where score 0 was bad and score 1 was defined as good. This can, of course, be extended to define any score values. Each input stimuli was assigned a score value and so it belonged to a certain class for the SVM. In the testing phase, we ask the SVM for the probability of the input signal to belong to each of the available classes. This in turn gives us the weights for a weighted average of the initially defined score values.

Optimizer

To find rendering parameter values, we use a standard Nelder-Mead (NM) optimizer [NM65]. NM optimization iteratively minimizes an unknown cost function of n variables and is commonly used in non-linear regression. We decided to use NM optimization instead of other widely used optimizers like genetic algorithms because NM is known to show good convergence characteristics if the cost function is reasonably smooth, as can be expected in our case. Little changes to rendering parameter values are likely to result in small changes to rendering output, which makes also the change of the visual appeal score of the SVM small. In contrast, genetic algorithms take many iterations to converge as they make no assumptions about the objective function, causing the number of iterations to increase exponentially with the number of parameters n as compared to only the polynomial complexity of NM [NM65].

Figure 5.3.: Original image versions used for SVM training (from MIT-Adobe FiveK Dataset)

5.4. Evaluation

To evaluate my approach, I consider two different rendering application scenarios. In Section 5.4.1, I investigate optimizing still-image photographs according to users' individual preferences. In Section 5.4.2, I evaluate our approach for optimizing overall rendering quality of short animation clips. For each application scenario, we train a separate SVM using exclusive visual content and separate participants than when we test the optimization framework.

5.4.1. Application Scenario: Photo Personalization

In the first optimization scenario saturation, brightness and contrast of a photo are varied to obtain aesthetically pleasing versions of the original image. The experimental set-up is based on the work in Chapter 3 and follows the same experimental procedures. Prior to performing the evaluation experiments, however, EEG data must be acquired for SVM training.

Classifier Training Phase

2 male and 8 female, healthy participants of an average age of 25 years and with normal or corrected-to-normal vision took part in collecting the EEG data needed to train the SVM. All participants had average experience with digital footage and no involvement in professional image/video rendering or editing. The participants were instructed orally and received a training session with a small image set but the same experimental set-up to prepare them for the procedure. It is important to note that these 10 participants who provided the data for SVM training were different from the ones that took part in the evaluation experiment, below.

The basic stimuli for the training phase consisted of 23 randomly selected images from the MIT-Adobe FiveK Dataset [BPCD11], Fig. 5.3. The database has a total of six versions for each image, the original photo plus five different, professional photographer-modified versions. This dataset was chosen because we wanted a publicly available dataset that had not only the original image, but professionally enhanced versions to teach the classifier what "good" enhancements are. We also deliberately chose a dataset with neutral images, because we wanted to measure the emotional response to the "look" of an image rather to its content.

Since all images in the database are aesthetically pleasing to a certain degree, we created two additional versions by either over-saturating or over-exposing them. This was necessary so that the support vector machine (SVM) could be trained to learn the differences between the brain's response to a visually appealing image (expertly retouched) and one that is not (over-saturated or over-exposed). To gather SVM training data, The participants were presented with the original photo, two of the expert-retouched aesthetic versions, as well as the over-saturated and over-exposed versions, totalling 5 versions per photo and 115 different images overall. Each participant was shown the same 115 images. The order in which the different photos were shown was randomized, with all versions of the same photo appearing after each other but also in random order. Each image was shown for a total of 2 seconds, followed by a fixation screen (gray background with a white dot in the center) shown for 700ms. The participants were instructed to mentally judge their preference for each image. At the end of each trial (all versions for one photo), the participants were shown all versions of the photo as thumbnails and asked to select the one they liked best. This was timed so as to not give them any opportunity to compare and analyse the images, but to quickly select one based on their initial preference. This task was given to focus and keep their attention on the images. We deliberately did not use their feedback for SVM training.

To train the SVM, we used one second of EEG data after each image appeared, totalling 1150 seconds of EEG recordings. The data was converted into time-frequency bands using the complex wavelet transform (Section 4.3.1), and the data from the first and last 1/4 second was discarded [MGM12]. In addition, a visual appeal score of 1 was assigned to the three versions from the FiveK dataset, and a score of 0 to the two over-saturated and over-exposed versions. To confirm the validity of the trained classifier I ran two tailed t-tests on the data A. The results are as follows:

1. Original vs. Bad Version 1 : $p < 0.0001$

2. Original vs. Bad Version 2: $p < 0.0001$

3. Bad Version 1 vs. Photographer Version 1: $p < 0.0001$

4. Bad Version 1 vs. Photographer Version 2: $p < 0.02$

5. Bad Version 2 vs. Photographer Version 1: $p < 0.0001$

6. Bad Version 2 vs. Photographer Version 2: $p < 0.0001$

Given the rejection of the null hypothesis in all cases there is sufficient evidence for the statistical significance of the results on which the classification is based. However, the results between photographers when compared to the bad versions vary since each photographer has a unique style of editing. However, given that all p-values are less than 0.05, each condition is statistically significantly different from the other. Once the SVM was trained with this data, the classifier was ready to categorize a single trial to calculate a visual appeal score.

Experiment

The method was evaluated with 15 users who did not participate in the SVM training phase. Their average age was 25 years, and they had no professional experience in image or video editing. The evaluation experiment was done on randomly selected photos from the MIT-Adobe FiveK Dataset [BPCD11] which had not been used for SVM training,see Appendix B. For each photo, the optimization loop was initialized with the original image version. To personally optimize the photo, the optimization loop was set to vary the three parameters saturation, brightness and contrast. The possible range for each parameter was set to allow for significant variations in image appearance but without becoming unnatural. For each photo, the user was shown subsequently optimized versions based on their EEG response while watching the subsequent image versions The users were asked to look at the rendered pictures and think about its aesthetic value. They were then shown a rating screen (1 - 5) and asked to rate the image based on how much they liked it. Optimization terminated either when it converged or after a maximum of 16 - 20 iterations. This was because for most people the images converged within a certain number of iterations after which the same image versions started to repeat. To be able to evaluate the SVM classifier-generated visual appeal scores, the scores generated for each image version during the experiment were stored and displayed to the experimenter during testing. After testing the framework with 15 users optimizing 12 photos, a perceptual study was conducted to compare the optimizer results with the photographer-enhanced versions for the images. The study was put online to allow a wider audience to evaluate the optimized versions. There were 8 original images (see Appendix B) shown along with the photographer-enhanced versions and some optimized-versions. The participants were asked to rate each image version from 1 - 5. There were a total of 90 participants for this study.

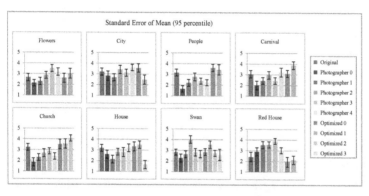

Figure 5.4.: Perceptual experiment results of optimized image enhanced versions vs. Photographer Enhanced Versions. There is no statistically significant difference in preferrence for EEG-optimized versions vs. photographer-enhanced versions

Results

The results from the optimization created distinct versions of the original images (Fig. 5.5, 5.6). These versions were unique to each individual and frequently different from the photographer enhanced versions. After each image optimization we had detailed discussions with the participants regarding the optimized images. All the participants preferred their own optimized version over the original image. Interestingly, often times it was not the accuracy of the image in terms of colour or details that the users were interested in but more often than not, their preference for the enhanced image was based on how it made them feel. We also discovered that this technique tends to work best for images that have the scope for aesthetic modifications like the flowers image (Fig. 5.6). For images that are about mundane everyday objects, like the car (Fig. 5.7), our approach tends to be limited in the aesthetic optimizations it can produce. One possible explanation for this is the lack of emotional response to some images of everyday objects.

To confirm the validity of the classifier scores, for each image version created during EEG-driven optimization we asked the users to rate it between 1(worst) - 5(best). We then compared their responses to the scores the classifier generated. Although there was a slight correlation, we could not determine a strong correlation between the classifier scores and the user ratings. One of the main problems with this comparison, is that the classifier scores are derived from a binary decision regarding the image. The classifier is trained to detect good and bad images from the EEG feedback. This binary decision is then converted into a weighted average score and so the scores from the classifier have a certain amount of noise, as do the user ratings. For example some images that were exactly the same in terms of parameters, were given drastically different ratings by users. Given this, it is difficult to determine a strong correlation between the scores and the user ratings.

To test the appeal of the results a perceptual study was conducted(see Experiment for details) to compare the optimized results with the photographer versions from the MIT-Adobe fivek dataset. The results as seen in Fig. 5.4 show that overall the optimized versions are competitive with the professional photographer-enhanced versions. We also ran two-tailed t-tests on the data to check for statistically significant differences in terms of preference for each image version. For each version the results were as follows:

1. Flowers: Photographer 0 and 1 were significantly worse, Photographer 3 and 4 were significantly better.

2. City : Photographer 0,1 and Optimized 1 were significantly worse whereas Photographer 4 and Optimized 0 were significantly better.

3. People: All Photographer versions were significantly worse whereas Optimized 0 was significantly better.

4. Carnival: Photographer 0, 1 and 3 were significantly worse, Photographer 4 and Optimized 1 were significantly better.

5. Church: All Photographer versions were significantly worse whereas all Optimized versions were significantly better.

6. House: Photographer 0, 1, 3 and Optimized 2 were significantly worse whereas Optimized 1 was significantly better.

7. Swan: Photographer 0 is significantly worse whereas Photographer 2 and Optimized 1 were significantly better.

8. Red House: Photographer 0, 1, 2, 3 and 4 were significantly better whereas Optimized 0 was significantly worse.

Overall, the average score for the EEG-optimized versions was approx. 3.1 as compared to 2.8 for the photographer-enhanced versions. As can be seen from the data in most cases the optimized versions and the photographer versions are statistically indistinguishable in terms of preference. I also ran a study with 50 participants comparing the optimized images against images created from random parameters. This study was conducted to ensure that our results were not due to random parameter generation. Here the average score of the optimized images was 3.6 compared to 2.2 for the random images thus showing that the optimized parameters are much better, on average, than randomly selected parameters.

5.4.2. Application: Guided Image Filter Parameter Optimization

In the second optimization scenario, I evaluated the performance of the technique when optimizing visual quality of a guided image-filtered animation sequence [BEM11]. Filtering noisy images is a fundamental image enhancement operation in video and image processing, but also in real-time global illumination rendering based on Monte Carlo sampling. The guided image filter is a powerful, edge-aware de-noising filter that uses additional model information such as normals and depth as guide to smooth out image noise while not affecting scene information. The guided image filter features three parameters, the filter radius plus two epsilon values that need to be selected and whose optimal values depend on scene characteristics. All three parameters affect the rendering result in different ways, controlling both surface smoothness and the amount of detail.

Classifier Training Phase

To collect SVM training data, 8 healthy participants of an average age of 25 years and with normal or corrected-to-normal vision took part. As training test data, we ray-traced the popular Crytek Sponza scene [Mei10], Fig.5.8(a) and the Sibenik Cathedral [DO02], Fig.5.8(b). We used a real-time global illumination ray tracer to create different versions of both scenes [BEM11]:

1. Four un-filtered sequences with 1, 4, 64 and 256 samples per pixel,

2. Six sequences using the guided image filter [HST10] with 1 and 4 samples per pixel, each with three different radii,

3. Four sequences using the á-Trous wavelet transform filter [DSHL10] with 1 and 4 samples per pixel, each with two different radii.

In total, 28 different animation sequence examples were used for recording the SVM training data. Each animation sequence was 3 seconds in length, and each sequence was shown 5 times to each participant to gather EEG data. To prepare them for the procedure the participants were instructed orally and received a practice run with a smaller video set but the same experimental set-up. After each animation was shown, the participants were asked to rate its quality on a scale from 1 (worst) to 5 (best). While we did not use this data, the task was designed to focus the participants on the stimuli being shown. The EEG data collected from these 8 participants was then used for training the classifier as explained in Section 4.3.1.

Experiment

The method was evaluated with 15 users who did not participate in the acquisition of the SVM training data. As test scene, we used a scene from the blender movie Sintel during evaluation Fig. 5.8 [Ble11]. The filter parameters to be optimized were radius, epsilon(normal) and epsilon(depth) [BEM11]. We chose to set the radius range between 2 and 32, and both epsilon values can vary within a limited range. The users were shown the original rendered sequences and subsequently the EEG-driven optimized versions. In this experiment, the optimization process terminated automatically when the variation of parameter values between subsequent iterations became too small. The iteration step with the highest EEG-derived score was selected as the final optimization result for each user.

5.4.2.1. Results

To evaluate the preference of the EEG-optimized videos to a general audience, we conducted a perceptual experiment with 23 participants. The participants were asked to rate 7 videos out of which 6 were optimized by the framework and one had been optimized manually by an expert. The participants had not been part of the training or testing phase. They were shown the animation sequences and were asked to rate each from 1(worst) to 5(best), based on the quality of each video. They were allowed to view each sequence as many times as needed to make a decision about the rating but were not informed about the parameters or if the video was manually optimized or EEG-optimized. We designed the experiment to ask the participants to rate the videos as opposed to pick one best version because we wanted to know how close together in terms of preference the different versions were. We ran a two tailed t-test on the data from these participants. The t-test probability is for the null-hypothesis P(H0) that the ratings of the optimized versions are from the same random population as for the manually optimized one A. As can be seen from Table 5.1 except for Optimized version 3 all the optimized versions are statistically indistinguishable from each other. The six optimized versions were from 6 different participants, and although some of the t-test numbers are smaller than others, the results show that for most of the optimized versions the ratings were statistically not significantly different from the manual version.

The results show that our EEG-optimized video sequences are visually as pleasing as an expert optimized sequence. More importantly, it is possible to determine the perceptual quality of a video sequence from single-trial EEG measurements without a reference video. This is especially interesting because videos have been known to be notoriously difficult to analyze using EEG techniques. Videos contain movement and rapid content changes which makes it very hard to determine whether EEG signals are due to quality or to changing video content. Since the method was tested with video content (Sintel) that the classifier had not been trained on, the results indicate that our approach

	Avg. Score	T-Test P(H0)
Manual	3.13	1.00
Optimized 0	2.39	0.06
Optimized 1	2.96	0.66
Optimized 2	3.04	0.82
Optimized 3	2.26	0.01
Optimized 4	2.61	0.10
Optimized 5	2.52	0.08

Table 5.1.: Comparison of user preference between the manually optimized parameters and six EEG-optimized versions created by five different users. The results show that there is no statistical significance in preference of manual over optimized versions.

is able to discriminate between visual quality and changing content. Also, in contrast to previous EEG studies [SBT[+]12, MLM12] that are based on detecting the occurrence of a certain event or sudden change in quality during video presentation, the animation sequences we used were of uniform quality i.e. no sudden 'event' like artifacts. Our experiment shows that EEG can also be used to assess overall visual quality, without the need of a reference, artifact detection, or sudden changes.

5.5. Discussion

For both evaluation scenarios, the SVM was trained using different participants and different visual content than in the evaluation experiments. The results show that (1) it is possible to use single-trial EEG measurements to assess the visual appeal of rendered still images as well as animations, and (2) the proposed approach is sufficiently robust across different users and content to allow for reliable optimization of rendering parameter values.

Depending on the type of rendering application, the "visual appeal" of an image or animation, as assessed by this approach, can correspond to general visual quality or to individual taste. The application scenario investigated in Sect. 5.4.1 concerns optimizing the visual aesthetics of the presented photos, according to each user's individual preferences. In contrast, the application scenario tested in Sect. 5.4.2 is about overall visual quality of the animated sequence shown, which was optimized similarly by the participants. Although this method is designed to work with arbitrary rendering algorithms, it is currently limited by the number of parameters that can reasonably be optimized simultaneously. We found that the number of iterations necessary until the result converges varies considerably between participants, taking between less than 1 minute to more than 5 minutes. Given the NM optimizer's polynomial complexity, increasing the number of variable parameters from 3 to 4 is likely to increase the time to convergence by about 50%. My experiments indicate that it requires at least one second of presentation time and recorded EEG data to reliably estimate the "visual appeal" of an image (in our experiments we showed each image for 2 seconds). In the current implementation, one iteration step takes an additional 30ms (images) to 45ms (videos) for data processing. With faster signal processing and SVM implementation, it is expected that this approach will be able to simultaneously optimize 6 or maybe even 7 parameters within reasonable time. Alternatively, the set of rendering parameters can be divided into subsets and optimized separately in sequence.

The experiments and methods presented in this chapter are an initial proof of concept for the use of EEG for measuring abstract concepts like aesthetics and personal preference for images. The methodology can be extended with the use of additional information about the underlying origins of the neural signals to optimize parameters based on specific brain functions. So, for example to optimize colour, the neural signal originating from the cortical area V4 could be used specifically instead of using an averaged signal [MZ97]. Similarly, research has shown cortical area V1 to be the origins of orientation perception [HR05]. The introduction of an additional step before optimization to extract activity of underlying brain areas will allow more accurate optimization of the parameters by using the neural response to each specific parameter change. It would also allow a better understanding of fundamental issues in graphics like edge detection, motion detection and orientation.

5.6. Summary

This chapter presents a novel approach for the optimization of rendering parameters based on single-trial EEG measurements. I show that it is possible to assess the visual appeal of a rendered still image as well as an animation from a user's EEG recording. This technique works with arbitrary visual content and can be employed to any visual rendering algorithm whose parameter settings affect rendering output. This work is an initial proof of concept for the use of EEG for evaluating abstract measures such as aesthetics. The use of EEG to measure a user's implicit visual and emotional response allows the direct quantification of the aesthetic value of an image. I demonstrate the applicability of my method for two different scenarios: general visual-quality enhancement, and individual photo personalization. Our EEG-based approach by-passes the need to explicitly quantify or define what qualities an appealing image possesses and requires no skill on the user's part. It is especially useful in cases where the user cannot express what he desires but is able to appreciate and identify with an appealing image when he sees it.

Finally, the results beg investigation of other, novel uses of EEG in computer graphics and visualization, e.g. to assess the aesthetic merits of non-photorealistic rendering, to make use of real-time implicit emotional feedback in games, visualization tasks and simulators, or to perceptually analyze the width and depth of the "Uncanny Valley".

(a) Original input image

(b) Optimized Version 1   (c) Optimized Version 2

(d) Photographer Version 1   (e) Photographer Version 2

Figure 5.5.: EEG-optimized results are unique for each individual and competitive in terms of visual appeal with the photographer enhanced versions.

(a) Original input image

(b) Optimized Version 1

(c) Optimized Version 2

(d) Photographer Version 1

(e) Photographer Version 2

Figure 5.6.: EEG-optimized results are unique for each individual and competitive in terms of visual appeal with the photographer enhanced versions.

(a) Original input image

(b) Optimized Version 1

(c) Optimized Version 2

(d) Photographer Version 1

(e) Photographer Version 2

Figure 5.7.: EEG-optimized results are limited by the content of the image and images of mundane objects do not optimize well.

(a) Crytek Sponza Sequence used for Training

(b) Sibenik Cathedral Sequence used for Training

(c) Original Sintel Frame

(d) Optimized Sintel Frame

Figure 5.8.: Scenes from animation sequences used for training and testing the EEG feedback optimization loop.

6. Conclusion and Future Directions

In this work I have presented several approaches to support the use of EEG for graphics applications. Chapter 3 presents initial experiments and analysis that shows that the covert (implicit) and overt (explicit) output of the human visual processing does differ, and in some cases this difference is striking. I also show that the brain responds very differently to not only different types of artifacts but also to artifacts specifically linked with motion. Artifacts linked with motion evoke a much stronger response in the brain. The experiments also show that it is possible to categorize artifacts based on how they are perceived. This provides information on the perception of videos which has previously not been modelled. This work also creates the possibility of shortening rendering times by eliminating computations that calculate image features which do not evoke a strong reaction in the brain as opposed to those which do. The brains response to artifacts is also essential for the modelling of masking algorithms for rendered image sequences.

Chapter 4 introduces a new method for the single-trial classification of typical IBR artifacts. We show that wavelets and an SVM are an effective way to deal with the problem of low signal-to-noise ratios inherent in EEG signals.

We also show that it is possible with a good degree of accuracy, to distinguish between different types of artifacts appearing in video stimuli from a single trial.

Chapter 5 presents a novel approach for the optimization of rendering parameters based on single-trial EEG measurements. I show that it is possible to assess the visual appeal of a rendered still image as well as an animation from a user's EEG recording. Our technique works with arbitrary visual content and can be employed to any visual rendering algorithm whose parameter settings affect rendering output. The use of EEG to measure a user's implicit visual and emotional response allows us to directly quantify the aesthetic value of an image. I demonstrate the applicability of this method for two different scenarios: general visual-quality enhancement, and individual photo personalization. My EEG-based approach by-passes the need to explicitly quantify or define what qualities an appealing image possesses and requires no skill on the user's part. It is especially useful in cases where the user cannot express what he desires but is able to appreciate and identify with an appealing image when he sees it.

The presented projects have shown that not only is it possible to determine the quality of an image or video using EEG, it is also possible to modify that quality in a direct feedback loop till an optimal solution is reached. Neural data constitutes a viable measure of aesthetic appeal for images and videos and for biofeedback for graphics applications; especially to analyse the perception of rendered image sequences.

This work provides an initial proof of concept for the use of EEG for solving graphics problems and creating novel interactive methods. A natural next step in this direction will be to decouple the EEG signal according to the underlying brain functionality and analyse the responses based on that [MML$^+$04]. Given this information it may be possible to more accurately determine the neural responses to edges, motion, colour and orientation, for example. This location data can then be used as another feature for the methods presented in this work for brain data analysis. For example, the pipeline presented in Chapter 5 could be modified to include the exact activity of underlying brain areas. The SVM could be trained and tested on activity from specific brain areas, and the optimization then based on weighted scores of the parameters to be optimized i.e. for optimization of colour, use activity from 'colour' cortical regions (V4 in the primary visual areas [MZ97]), 'edge' brain areas to optimize contrast etc.

An analysis of the underlying origins of the neural signals will also help in the better understanding of the perception of artifacts linked with motion as described in Chapter 3. Research has shown that the visual area V5, also known as visual area MT (middle temporal) is thought to play a major role in the perception of motion [BB05]. A separation of and analysis of the neural signal originating from this region will allow for a better modelling of motion. Interestingly, research has shown activation in the MT region even while viewing static images with implied motion [KK00]. This may be particularly useful for graphics researchers and animators for modelling motion.

My contributions pave the way for novel, exciting combinations of computer graphics and EEG. There exist many graphics problems that can benefit from its use. For example, it is ideally suited for the quality assessment of 3D images and videos. Similarly, the Uncanny Valley has been a long discussed hypothesis from a graphics perspective. EEG data provides us with the possibility of quantifying and predicting this Uncanny Valley effect. Another interesting area of research is the automatic changing of a virtual reality environment based on direct neural feedback.

By the time this thesis is written, further research inspired by the approaches we presented has been published. Anton et al. [ALA+13] use EEG and self-assessment tools to explore the neural and emotional components of speech quality perception of reverberant speech, aiming at gaining new insights into human speech quality perception in complex listening environments. Tomkin et al. [TKK+13], instead of looking at traditional rendering artifacts (Chapter 3), look at seven transitional artifacts in videos, from movie cuts and dissolves to image-based warps and virtual camera transitions. Related to our methodology for image and video quality assessment presented in Chapter 3 Arndt et al. [AAS+14] describe a set of experiments to systematically examine the relation between visual and audiovisual quality, using the P300 components of ERP's. Mehta et al. [MK14] present a framework to assess the subjective perception of audio quality using EEG data. Similarly, Laghari et al. [GAS+13] computed an electroencephalography (EEG) feature based on the coupling between delta and beta EEG frequency bands showing an increase in delta and beta coupling corresponding to a decrease in the speech quality levels. They also computed neural correlates of subjective affective scores (arousal and valence) which showed inverse proportionality with EEG features. Their results corroborate that emotions play a significant role in human quality and perception. In a different direction George et al. [GID14] couple EEG data with neural networks to identify simple images viewed by a human participant. Similarly, Khasnobish et al. [KKT$^+$13] propose a method to recognize object shapes from EEG data while a subject is exploring the same object using visual and tactile means. Content prediction from EEG data of what the subject is viewing or touching is particularly interesting for rendering applications since it allows us to understand how a rendered object is being perceived.

EEG has a huge potential for a variety of applications in graphics, and I hope the contributions presented here will have a significant impact in introducing EEG as a novel modality for graphics research.

A. Two-Tailed T-Test

The two-tailed t-test is used to determine if two populations originate from the same random distribution. It is applied to compare whether the average difference between two groups is really significant or if it is due instead to random chance. When a test of significance is used to compare two groups we usually start with the null hypothesis that there is no difference between the populations from which the data comes. If this hypothesis is not true the alternative hypothesis must be true i.e., that there is a difference. In a two data group case, the usual null hypothesis is that the two population means are equal, usually written as H0 :

$$\mu_1(\text{population}_1) = \mu_2(\text{population}_2)$$

where the symbol H0 indicates the null hypothesis. The typical alternative hypothesis is that the two population means are unequal i.e.

$$H1 : \mu_1 \neq \mu_2$$

The 't' statistic determines the difference between the data means (in either direction) divided by the (estimated) standard error of that difference. Since the null hypothesis specifies no direction for the difference nor does the alternative hypothesis, and so we have a two tailed test [BB$^+$94]. The null hypothesis is generally assumed to be true until evidence indicates otherwise. The two-tailed t statistic is calculated as [Urd01]:

1. The average of both sample (observed averages) which are represented as:

$$\bar{X}_1 \text{ and } \bar{X}_2$$

2. The standard deviation (SD) of both averages which is represented as:

$$S_1 \text{ and } S_2$$

3. The number of observations in both populations, represented as

$$n_1 \text{ and } n_2$$

The test statistic for testing

$$H_0 : \mu_X = \mu_Y \text{ vs. } H_1 : \mu_X \neq \mu_Y$$

then is:

$$t = \frac{\bar{X}_1 - \bar{X}_2}{\sqrt{S_1^2/n_1 + S_2^2/n_2}}$$

Once the t-value has been calculated, we can determine the 'p-value' which is the probability that both random variables are from the same population, i.e. it gives us the probability that the sample sets are from the same random distribution. The p–value is derived from the integration of the probability distribution function (PDF) for values from -inf to -t and t to inf or one minus the integral of the PDF from -t to t. Typically, in statistics, if the p-value is less than or equal to a specific cut-off value the null hypothesis is rejected and retained otherwise. This cut-off value is called the significance level of a test, and the symbol alpha (α) is used to denote it, with the conventional alpha being 0.05 [Fis34]. The phrase 'statistically significant' is used at the 0.05 level, when the p-value is less than or equal to 0.05. Once the t-value has been calculated the p-value can be determined using a chi square distribution table.

B. Test Results for Neural feedback loop

(a) Original Swan Image

(b) EEG-Optimized versions

(c) Photographer enhanced versions

Figure B.1.: Swan test image shown to participants for optimization

(a) Original Church Image

(b) EEG-optimized versions

(c) Photographer enhanced versions

Figure B.2.: Church test image shown to participants for optimization

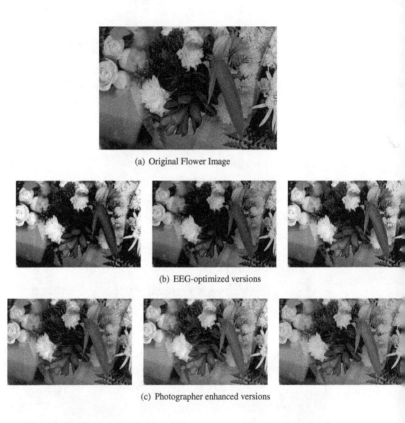

(a) Original Flower Image

(b) EEG-optimized versions

(c) Photographer enhanced versions

Figure B.3.: Flower test image shown to participants for optimization

(a) Original Gas Station Image

(b) EEG-optimized versions

(c) Photographer enhanced versions

Figure B.4.: Gas station test image shown to participants for optimization

(a) Original House Image

(b) EEG-optimized versions

(c) Photographer enhanced versions

Figure B.5.: House test image shown to participants for optimization

(a) Original Carnival Image

(b) EEG-optimized versions

(c) Photographer enhanced versions

Figure B.6.: Carnival test image shown to participants for optimization

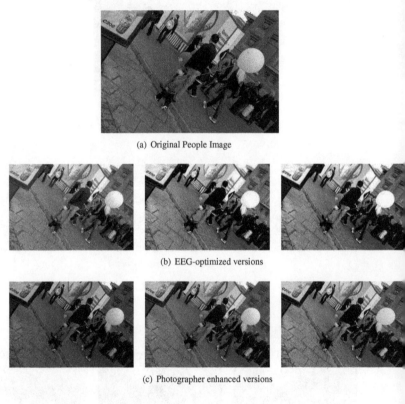

(a) Original People Image

(b) EEG-optimized versions

(c) Photographer enhanced versions

Figure B.7.: People test image shown to participants for optimization

References

[AAS+14] Sebastian Arndt, J Antons, Robert Schleicher, S Moller, and Gabriel Curio. Using electroencephalography to measure perceived video quality. 2014.

[ABM08] R.G. Adams, G.S. Bahr, and B. Moreno. Brain computer interfaces: psychology and pragmatic perspectives for the future. 2008.

[ALA+13] J-N Antons, KUR Laghari, Sebastian Arndt, Robert Schleicher, S Moller, D O'Shaughnessy, and Tiago H Falk. Cognitive, affective, and experience correlates of speech quality perception in complex listening conditions. In *Acoustics, Speech and Signal Processing (ICASSP), 2013 IEEE International Conference on*, pages 3672–3676. IEEE, 2013.

[APM⁺11] E. W. Anderson, K. C. Potter, L. E. Matzen, J. F. Shepherd, G. A. Preston, and C. T. Silva. A user study of visualization effectiveness using eeg and cognitive load. *Computer Graphics Forum*, 30(3):791–800, 2011.

[Bay03] Jessica D Bayliss. Use of the evoked potential p3 component for control in a virtual apartment. *Neural Systems and Rehabilitation Engineering, IEEE Transactions on*, 11(2):113–116, 2003.

[BB⁺94] J Martin Bland, DG Bland, et al. Statistics notes: One and two sided tests of significance. *Bmj*, 309(6949):248, 1994.

[BB05] Richard T Born and David C Bradley. Structure and function of visual area mt. *Annu. Rev. Neurosci.*, 28:157–189, 2005.

[BDS12] Adriaan Barria, Ann Doomsa, and Peter Schelkensa. The near shift-invariance of the dual-tree complex wavelet transform revisited. *Journal of Mathematical Analysis and Applications*, 389:1303–1314, May 2012.

[BEM11] Pablo Bauszat, Martin Eisemann, and Marcus Magnor. Guided image filtering for interactive high-
quality global illumination. *Computer Graphics Forum (Proc. of Eurographics Symposium on Rendering (EGSR))*, 30(4):1361–1368, June 2011.

[BHVH12] Brian D Berman, Silvina G Horovitz, Gaurav
Venkataraman, and Mark Hallett. Self-modulation of
primary motor cortex activity with motor and motor
imagery tasks using real-time fmri-based neurofeed-
back. *Neuroimage*, 59(2):917–925, 2012.

[bio13] Biosemi activetwo system, 2013. http://www.
biosemi.com/products.htm.

[Ble11] Blender Foundation. Sintel. http://www.
sintel.org/, 2011.

[Bos06] Danny Oude Bos. Eeg-based emotion recognition.
The Influence of Visual and Auditory Stimuli, 2006.

[BPCD11] V. Bychkovsky, S. Paris, E. Chan, and F. Durand.
Learning photographic global tonal adjustment with
a database of input/output image pairs. In *Computer*

Vision and Pattern Recognition (CVPR), 2011 IEEE Conference on, pages 97–104. IEEE, 2011.

[CA04] James A Coan and John J.B Allen. Frontal eeg asymmetry as a moderator and mediator of emotion. *Biological Psychology*, 67(1–2):7 – 50, 2004.

[CCV03] Paulo Cezar, Pinto Carvalho, and Luiz Velho. Mathematical optimization in graphics and vision. In *Course Notes Siggraph*, 2003.

[CGL⁺08] Forrester Cole, Aleksey Golovinskiy, Alex Limpaecher, Heather Stoddart Barros, Adam Finkelstein, Thomas Funkhouser, and Szymon Rusinkiewicz. Where do people draw lines? *ACM Transactions on Graphics (Proc. SIGGRAPH)*, 27(3), August 2008.

[CKGP06] G. Chanel, J. Kronegg, D. Grandjean, and T. Pun. Emotion assessment: Arousal evaluation using eegs and peripheral physiological signals. *Multimedia content representation, classification and security*, pages 530–537, 2006.

[CL11] Chih-Chung Chang and Chih-Jen Lin. LIBSVM: A library for support vector machines. *ACM Transactions on Intelligent Systems and Technology*, 2:27:1–27:27, 2011.

[CMMN99] John K Chapin, Karen A Moxon, Ronald S Markowitz, and Miguel AL Nicolelis. Real-time control of a robot arm using simultaneously recorded neurons in the motor cortex. *Nature neuroscience*, 2(7):664–670, 1999.

[DO02] Marko Dabrovic and Mihovil Odak. Sibenik Cathedral. `http://http://hdri.cgtechniques.com/~sibenik2/download`, 2002.

[DSHL10] Holger Dammertz, Daniel Sewtz, Johannes Hanika, and Hendrik P. A. Lensch. Edge-avoiding a-trous wavelet transform for fast global illumination filtering. In *Proceedings of the Conference on High Performance Graphics*, HPG '10, pages 67–75, Aire-la-Ville, Switzerland, Switzerland, 2010. Eurographics Association.

[Emo12] Emotiv. Epoc neuroheadset. http://www.emotiv.com/store/hardware/epoc-bci/epoc-neuroheadset/, 2012.

[Fec48] Gustav Theodor Fechner. Elements of psychophysics, 1860. 1948.

[FHC04] Charlie D Frowd, Peter JB Hancock, and Derek Carson. Evofit: A holistic, evolutionary facial imaging technique for creating composites. *ACM Transactions on Applied Perception (TAP)*, 1(1):19–39, 2004.

[Fis34] Ronald Aylmer Fisher. Statistical methods for research workers. 1934.

[FKH67] Irwin Feinberg, Richard L Koresko, and Naomi Heller. Eeg sleep patterns as a function of normal and pathological aging in man. *Journal of psychiatric research*, 5(2):107–144, 1967.

[FLR09] Andrea Finke, Alexander Lenhardt, and Helge Ritter. The mindgame: a p300-based brain–computer interface game. *Neural Networks*, 22(9):1329–1333, 2009.

[FP04] Jean-Philippe Farrugia and Bernard Péroche. A progressive rendering algorithm using an adaptive perceptually based image metric. *Computer Graphics Forum*, 23:605–614, 2004.

[FSPG96] A. J. Ferwerda, P. Shiley, N.S. Pattanaik, and P.D. Greenberg. A model of visual adaptation for realistic image synthesis. In *Proc. ACM SIGGRAPH*, pages 249–258, 1996.

[GAL90] Douglas S Goodin, Michael J Aminoff, and Kenneth D Laxer. Detection of epileptiform activity by different noninvasive eeg methods in complex partial epilepsy. *Annals of neurology*, 27(3):330–334, 1990.

[GAS$^+$13] Rishabh Gupta, Jan-Niklas Antons, Robert Schleicher, Sebastian Moller, Tiago H Falk, et al. Objective characterization of human behavioural characteristics for qoe assessment: A pilot study on the use of electroencephalography features. In *Globecom Workshops (GC Wkshps), 2013 IEEE*, pages 1168–1173. IEEE, 2013.

[Ges13] George A Gescheider. *Psychophysics: the fundamentals*. Psychology Press, 2013.

[GG01] B. Gooch and A. Gooch. *Non-photorealistic rendering*, volume 201. AK Peters, 2001.

[GH79] Richard L Gregory and Priscilla Heard. Border locking and the café wall illusion. *Perception*, 8(4):365–380, 1979.

[GID14] Kiran George, Adrian Iniguez, and Hayden Donze. Sensing and decoding of visual stimuli using commercial brain computer interface technology. In *Instrumentation and Measurement Technology Conference (I2MTC) Proceedings, 2014 IEEE International*, pages 1102–1104. IEEE, 2014.

[Haa10] Alfred Haar. On the theory of orthogonal function systems. *Math. Ann*, 69:331–371, 1910.

[HBZ89] RH Hess, CL Baker, and J Zihl. The" motion-blind" patient: Low-level spatial and temporal filters. *The Journal of Neuroscience*, 9(5):1628–1640, 1989.

[HČA+12] R. Herzog, M. Čadík, T.O. Aydčin, K.I. Kim, K. Myszkowski, and H.P. Seidel. Norm: No-reference image quality metric for realistic image synthesis. In *Computer Graphics Forum*, volume 31, pages 545–554. Wiley Online Library, 2012.

[HDR08] R. Horlings, D. Datcu, and L.J.M. Rothkrantz. Emotion recognition using brain activity. In *Proceedings of the 9th International Conference on Computer Systems and Technologies and Workshop for PhD Students in Computing*, page 6. ACM, 2008.

[Her10] Aaron Hertzmann. Non-photorealistic rendering and the science of art. In *Proceedings of the 8th International Symposium on Non-Photorealistic Animation and Rendering*, NPAR '10, pages 147–157, 2010.

[HKK12] Sung Ju Hwang, Ashish Kapoor, and Sing Bing Kang. Context-based automatic local image enhancement. In *Computer Vision–ECCV 2012*, pages 569–582. Springer, 2012.

[HR05] John-Dylan Haynes and Geraint Rees. Predicting the orientation of invisible stimuli from activity in human primary visual cortex. *Nature neuroscience*, 8(5):686–691, 2005.

[HST10] Kaiming He, Jian Sun, and Xiaoou Tang. Guided image filtering. In *Proceedings of the 11th European conference on Computer vision: Part I*, ECCV'10, pages 1–14, Berlin, Heidelberg, 2010. Springer-Verlag.

[INC⁺06] T. Isenberg, P. Neumann, S. Carpendale, M.C. Sousa, and J.A. Jorge. Non-photorealistic rendering in context: an observational study. In *Proceedings of the 4th international symposium on Non-photorealistic animation and rendering*, pages 115–126. ACM, 2006.

[Int06] International Telecommunication Union. Mean opinion score (MOS) terminology. In *ITU-T Recommendation*, page P.800.1, 2006.

[KFC⁺10] Jaroslav Křivánek, Marcos Fajardo, Per H. Christensen, Eric Tabellion, Michael Bunnell, David Larsson, and Anton Kaplanyan. Global illumination across industries. In *ACM SIGGRAPH 2010 Courses*, SIGGRAPH '10, New York, NY, USA, 2010. ACM.

[KK00] Zoe Kourtzi and Nancy Kanwisher. Activation in human mt/mst by static images with implied motion. *Journal of cognitive neuroscience*, 12(1):48–55, 2000.

[KKT+13] Anwesha Khasnobish, Amit Konar, DN Tibarewala, Saugat Bhattacharyya, and Ramadoss Janarthanan. Object shape recognition from eeg signals during tactile and visual exploration. In *Pattern Recognition and Machine Intelligence*, pages 459–464. Springer, 2013.

[KLW12] L. Kaufman, D. Lischinski, and M. Werman. Content-aware automatic photo enhancement. In *Computer Graphics Forum*. Wiley Online Library, 2012.

[KNPG08] Kendrick N Kay, Thomas Naselaris, Ryan J Prenger, and Jack L Gallant. Identifying natural images from human brain activity. *Nature*, 452(7185):352–355, 2008.

[KPC93] John K. Kawai, James S. Painter, and Michael F. Cohen. Radioptimization: goal based rendering. In *Proceedings of the 20th annual conference on Computer graphics and interactive techniques*, SIGGRAPH '93, pages 147–154, New York, NY, USA, 1993. ACM.

[KST08] Ashish Kapoor, Pradeep Shenoy, and Desney Tan. Combining brain computer interfaces with vision for object categorization. In *Computer Vision and Pattern Recognition, 2008. CVPR 2008. IEEE Conference on*, pages 1–8. IEEE, 2008.

[KT05] Yukiyasu Kamitani and Frank Tong. Decoding the visual and subjective contents of the human brain. *Nature neuroscience*, 8(5):679–685, 2005.

[KT07] C. Koch and N. Tsuchiya. Attention and consciousness: two distinct brain processes. *Trends in Cognitive Sciences*, 11(1):16–22, 2007.

[LGM13] Anatole Lécuyer, Laurent George, and Maud Marchal. Toward adaptive VR simulators combining visual, haptic, and brain-computer interfaces. *IEEE*

Computer Graphics and Applications, 33(5):18–23, 2013.

[LH01] David Luebke and Benjamin Hallen. Perceptually driven simplification for interactive rendering, 2001.

[LM11] L. Lindemann and M. Magnor. Assessing the quality of compressed images using EEG. In *Proc. IEEE International Conference on Image Processing (ICIP)*, pages 3170–3173, 2011.

[LN06] Mikhail A. Lebedev and Miguel A.L. Nicolelis. Brain–machine interfaces: past, present and future. *Trends in Neurosciences*, 29(9):536 – 546, 2006.

[Luc05] S. J. Luck. *An Introduction to Event-Related Potentials and Their Neural Origins (Chapter 1)*. MIT Press, Cambridge, 2005.

[LWM11] L. Lindemann, S. Wenger, and M. Magnor. Evaluation of video artifact perception using event-related potentials. *ACM Applied Perception in Computer Graphics and Visualization (APGV)*, pages 1–5, 2011.

[MAB+97] J. Marks, B. Andalman, P.A. Beardsley, W. Free-
man, S. Gibson, J. Hodgins, T. Kang, B. Mirtich,
H. Pfister, W. Ruml, et al. Design galleries: A
general approach to setting parameters for computer graphics and animation. In *Proceedings of
the 24th annual conference on Computer graphics
and interactive techniques*, pages 389–400. ACM
Press/Addison-Wesley Publishing Co., 1997.

[MBB12] Rachel McDonnell, Martin Breidt, and Heinrich H.
Bülthoff. Render me real?: Investigating the effect
of render style on the perception of animated virtual
humans. *ACM Trans. Graph.*, 31(4):91:1–91:11, July
2012.

[McN01] Ann McNamara. Visual perception in realistic image
synthesis. *Comput. Graph. Forum*, 20(4):211–224,
2001.

[Mei10] Frank Meinl. Crytek Sponza Atrium.
`http://www.crytek.com/cryengine/`
`cryengine3/downloads`, 2010.

[MGM12] Maryam Mustafa, Stefan Guthe, and Marcus Magnor. Single trial EEG classification of artifacts in videos. *ACM Transactions on Applied Perception (TAP)*, 9(3):12:1–12:15, July 2012.

[MGPF99] Johannes Müller-Gerking, Gert Pfurtscheller, and Henrik Flyvbjerg. Designing optimal spatial filters for single-trial eeg classification in a movement task. *Clinical neurophysiology*, 110(5):787–798, 1999.

[MK14] Ketan Mehta and Jorg Kliewer. Assessing subjective perception of audio quality by measuring the information flow on the brain-response channel. In *Acoustics, Speech and Signal Processing (ICASSP), 2014 IEEE International Conference on*, pages 5884–5888. IEEE, 2014.

[MLHB92] CM Michel, D Lehmann, B Henggeler, and D Brandeis. Localization of the sources of eeg delta, theta, alpha and beta frequency bands using the fft dipole approximation. *Electroencephalography and clinical neurophysiology*, 82(1):38–44, 1992.

[MLM12] Maryam Mustafa, Lea Lindemann, and Marcus Magnor. EEG analysis of implicit human visual perception. In *Proc. ACM Human Factors in Computing Systems (CHI) 2012*, May 2012.

[MM14] Maryam Mustafa and Marcus Magnor. Electroencephalographics: Making waves in computer graphics research. 2014.

[MMBH10] A. McNamara, K. Mania, M. Banks, and C. Healey. Perceptually-motivated graphics, visualization and 3D displays. In *Proc. ACM SIGGRAPH*, pages 1–159, 2010.

[MML^{+}04] Christoph M. Michel, Micah M. Murray, Göran Lantz, Sara Gonzalez, Laurent Spinelli, and Rolando Grave de Peralta. {EEG} source imaging. *Clinical Neurophysiology*, 115(10):2195 – 2222, 2004.

[MN84] Suzanne P McKee and Ken Nakayama. The detection of motion in the peripheral visual field. *Vision research*, 24(1):25–32, 1984.

[MRN⁺08] M Murugappan, M Rizon, R Nagarajan, S Yaacob, D Hazry, and I Zunaidi. Time-frequency analysis of eeg signals for human emotion detection. In *4th Kuala Lumpur International Conference on Biomedical Engineering 2008*, pages 262–265. Springer, 2008.

[Mul73] Thomas Mulholland. Objective eeg methods for studying covert shifts of visual attention. In *The psychophysiology of thinking*, pages 109–151. Academic Press New York, 1973.

[MVL00] Jurriaan D Mulder and Robert Van Liere. Fast perception-based depth of field rendering. In *Proceedings of the ACM symposium on Virtual reality software and technology*, pages 129–133. ACM, 2000.

[MZ97] DJ McKeefry and S Zeki. The position and topography of the human colour centre as revealed by functional magnetic resonance imaging. *Brain*, 120(12):2229–2242, 1997.

[N⁺02] CP Niemic et al. Studies of emotion: A theoretical and empirical review of psychophysiological studies of emotion. *Journal of Undergraduate Research*, 1(1):15–18, 2002.

[NM65] J.A. Nelder and R. Mead. A simplex method for function minimization. *The computer journal*, 7(4):308–313, 1965.

[NPK⁺09] Thomas Naselaris, Ryan J. Prenger, Kendrick N. Kay, Michael Oliver, and Jack L. Gallant. Bayesian reconstruction of natural images from human brain activity. *Neuron*, 63(6):902 – 915, 2009.

[OPOZ06] Hannu Olkkonen, Peitsa Pesola, Juuso Olkkonen, and Hui Zhou. Hilbert transform assisted complex wavelet transform for neuroelectric signal analysis. *Journal of Neuroscience Methods*, 151:106–113, March 2006.

[OSB99] Alan V. Oppenheim, Ronald W. Schafer, and John R. Buck. *Discrete-time signal processing (2nd ed.)*. Prentice-Hall, Inc., Upper Saddle River, NJ, USA, 1999.

[PBSDS06] G Pfurtscheller, C Brunner, A Schlögl, and FH Lopes Da Silva. Mu rhythm (de) synchronization and eeg single-trial classification of different motor imagery tasks. *Neuroimage*, 31(1):153–159, 2006.

[PLZ⁺09] N. Ponomarenko, V. Lukin, A. Zelensky, K. Egiazarian, J. Astola, M. Carli, and F. Battisti. A database for evaluation of full-reference visual quality assessment metrics. *Advances of Modern Radioelectronics*, 10(10):30–45, 2009.

[RHBS07] G.A. Rousselet, J.S. Husk, P.J. Bennett, and A.B. Sekuler. Single-trial eeg dynamics of object and face visual processing. *NeuroImage*, (36):843–862, 2007.

[RK87] Charles F Reynolds and David J Kupfer. Sleep research in affective illness: state of the art circa 1987. *Sleep: Journal of Sleep Research & Sleep Medicine*, 1987.

[RL00] Szymon Rusinkiewicz and Marc Levoy. QSplat: A multiresolution point rendering system for large meshes. In *Proceedings of ACM SIGGRAPH 2000*, pages 343–352, July 2000.

[RMGP00] Herbert Ramoser, Johannes Muller-Gerking, and Gert Pfurtscheller. Optimal spatial filtering of single trial eeg during imagined hand movement. *Rehabilitation Engineering, IEEE Transactions on*, 8(4):441–446, 2000.

[SAKK05] Abdulhamit Subasi, Ahmet Alkan, Etem Koklukaya, and M. Kemal Kiymik. Wavelet neural network classification of eeg signals by using ar model with mle preprocessing. *Neural Netw.*, 18(7):985–997, September 2005.

[SB10] Kalpana Seshadrinathan and Alan Conrad Bovik. Motion tuned spatio-temporal quality assessment of natural videos. *Image Processing, IEEE Transactions on*, 19(2):335–350, 2010.

[SBT+12] S. Scholler, S. Bosse, M.S. Treder, B. Blankertz, G. Curio, K.R. Muller, and T. Wiegand. Toward a direct measure of video quality perception using eeg. *Image Processing, IEEE Transactions on*, 21(5):2619–2629, 2012.

[SDS⁺93] C. Schoeneman, J. Dorsey, B. Smits, J. Arvo, and D. Greenberg. Painting with light. In *Proceedings of the 20th annual conference on Computer graphics and interactive techniques*, pages 143–146. ACM, 1993.

[SH06] Rezwan Sayeed and Toby Howard. State of the art non-photorealistic rendering (npr) techniques. In *Theory and Practice of Computer Graphics 2006*, pages 89–98, 2006.

[Sim91] Karl Sims. Artificial evolution for computer graphics. *SIGGRAPH Comput. Graph.*, 25(4):319–328, July 1991.

[SL01] R. Shacked and D. Lischinski. Automatic lighting design using a perceptual quality metric. In *Computer graphics forum*, volume 20, pages 215–227. Wiley Online Library, 2001.

[SMH⁺04] Gerwin Schalk, Dennis J McFarland, Thilo Hinterberger, Niels Birbaumer, and Jonathan R Wolpaw. Bci2000: a general-purpose brain-computer interface (bci) system. *Biomedical Engineering, IEEE Transactions on*, 51(6):1034–1043, 2004.

[SPW⁺10] Paul Sajda, Eric Pohlmeyer, Jun Wang, Lucas C Parra, Christoforos Christoforou, Jacek Dmochowski, Barbara Hanna, Claus Bahlmann, Maneesh Kumar Singh, and Shih-Fu Chang. In a blink of an eye and a switch of a transistor: cortically coupled computer vision. *Proceedings of the IEEE*, 98(3):462–478, 2010.

[SRP98] Sara C Sereno, Keith Rayner, and Michael I Posner. Establishing a time-line of word recognition: evidence from eye movements and event-related potentials. *Neuroreport*, 9(10):2195–2200, 1998.

[SS00] Wim Sweldens and Peter Schroder. Building your own wavelets at home. *Computer*, (1995:5):15–87, 2000.

[SSS06] N. Snavely, M.S. Seitz, and R. Szeliski. Photo tourism: exploring photo collections in 3D. *ACM Trans. Graph.*, 25:835–846, 2006.

[ST01] Louis A Schmidt and Laurel J Trainor. Frontal brain electrical activity (eeg) distinguishes valence and intensity of musical emotions. *Cognition & Emotion*, 15(4):487–500, 2001.

[ST08] P. Shenoy and D.S. Tan. Human-aided computing: utilizing implicit human processing to classify images. pages 845–854, 2008.

[SYH⁺07] Cameron Sheikholeslami, Han Yuan, Eric J He, Xiaoxiao Bai, Lin Yang, and Bin He. A high resolution eeg study of dynamic brain activity during video game play. In *Engineering in Medicine and Biology Society, 2007. EMBS 2007. 29th Annual International Conference of the IEEE*, pages 2489–2491. IEEE, 2007.

[TDH90] Andrew J Tomarken, Richard J Davidson, and Jeffrey B Henriques. Resting frontal brain asymmetry predicts affective responses to films. *Journal of personality and social psychology*, 59(4):791, 1990.

[TKK⁺13] James Tompkin, Min H Kim, Kwang In Kim, Jan Kautz, and Christian Theobalt. Preference and artifact analysis for video transitions of places. *ACM Transactions on Applied Perception (TAP)*, 10(3):13, 2013.

[Urd01] Timothy C Urdan. *Statistics in plain English*. Psychology Press, 2001.

[VCL⁺11] P. Vangorp, G. Chaurasia, P.-Y. Laffont, R. W. Fleming, and G. Drettakis. Perception of visual artifacts in image-based rendering of facades. *Computer Graphics Forum*, 30:1241–1250, 2011.

[WB06] Z. Wang and A.C. Bovik. Modern image quality assessment. *Synthesis Lectures on Image, Video, and Multimedia Processing*, 2(1):1–156, 2006.

[WPH⁺09] Jun Wang, Eric Pohlmeyer, Barbara Hanna, Yu-Gang Jiang, Paul Sajda, and Shih-Fu Chang. Brain state decoding for rapid image retrieval. In *Proceedings of the 17th ACM International Conference on Multimedia*, MM '09, pages 945–954, New York, NY, USA, 2009. ACM.